"This brilliant work will teacl [barcode] convince you. With a sense of [obscured] age, challenge, and teach us to cultivate and pass on to our young generations a lasting legacy of prayer."

—ESTHER ILNISKY,
founder of the Children's Global Prayer Movement
and of Esther Network International

"*Prayer-Saturated Kids* is an inspiring and practical resource for parents and teachers who want to cover this generation of children in prayer, pass on a legacy of faith, and equip them to deal confidently and triumphantly with the great challenges they face in today's world."

—CHERI FULLER, international speaker,
author of *Opening Your Child's Spiritual Windows*
and *When Children Pray*

"Reading *Prayer-Saturated Kids* has made me thirsty to pray with and bless our grandchildren more. The practical ideas and stories are stimulating and motivating. It's exciting to contemplate what could happen if we grandparents, parents, and congregations were to catch the vision of this book!"

—GAIL MACDONALD, pastor's wife, author of *High Call, High Privilege*

PRAYER
SATURATED
KIDS

EQUIPPING AND EMPOWERING CHILDREN
IN PRAYER

CHERYL SACKS
ARLYN LAWRENCE

NavPress is the publishing ministry of The Navigators, an international Christian organization and leader in personal spiritual development. NavPress is committed to helping people grow spiritually and enjoy lives of meaning and hope through personal and group resources that are biblically rooted, culturally relevant, and highly practical.

For a free catalog go to www.NavPress.com
or call 1.800.366.7788 in the United States or 1.800.839.4769 in Canada.

ISBN-13: 978-1-60006-136-3
ISBN-10: 1-60006-136-2

Cover design by The DesignWorks Group, Jason Gabbert, www.thedesignworksgroup.com
Cover image by IndexStock, istock
Creative Team: Dave Wilson, Susan Martins Miller, Kathy Mosier, Darla Hightower, Arvid Wallen, Pat Reinheimer

Visit the *Pray!* website at www.praymag.com.

Some of the anecdotal illustrations in this book are true to life and are included with the permission of the persons involved. All other illustrations are composites of real situations, and any resemblance to people living or dead is coincidental.

Unless otherwise identified, all Scripture quotations in this publication are taken from the HOLY BIBLE: NEW INTERNATIONAL VERSION® (NIV®). Copyright © 1973, 1978, 1984 by International Bible Society. Used by permission of Zondervan Publishing House. All rights reserved. Other versions used include: the *Holy Bible, New Living Translation* (NLT), copyright © 1996, 2004. Used by permission of Tyndale House Publishers, Inc., Wheaton, Illinois 60189. All rights reserved; the *English Standard Version* (ESV), copyright © 2001 by Crossway Bibles, a division of Good News Publishers. Used by permission. All rights reserved; the *Amplified New Testament* (AMP), © The Lockman Foundation 1954, 1958; the *Amplified New Testament* (AMP), © The Lockman Foundation 1954, 1958; and the *King James Version* (KJV).

Sacks, Cheryl.
   Prayer-saturated kids : equipping and empowering children in prayer / Cheryl Sacks and Arlyn Lawrence.
      p. cm.
   Includes bibliographical references.
   ISBN 978-1-60006-136-3
   1. Family--Religious life. 2. Prayer--Christianity. I. Lawrence, Arlyn. II. Title.
   BV4526.3.S24 2007
   248.3'2085--dc22
                                        2007004854
Printed in the United States of America

3 4 5 6 7 8 / 12 11 10 09

This book is lovingly and prayerfully dedicated

to our children:

Nicole and her husband, Marco;

Tyler, Heather, Hayley, Timothy, and Hillary

CONTENTS

ACKNOWLEDGMENTS

We'd like to thank our husbands—Hal and Doug—for their encouragement, prayers, and support, and for their willingness to go above and beyond the call of duty even when it meant laundry, meals, dishes, and chauffeuring kids while we wrote this book.

We'd also like to thank our children, who at times have taught us more about prayer than we've taught them!

We are deeply indebted to our church families—Word of Grace Church and Destiny City Church—who have loved us, supported us, equipped us, and poured into our (and our children's) lives.

We are grateful to our developmental editor, Susan Martins Miller, and the editorial staff at *Pray!* Books/NavPress for their expertise in bringing this book to fruition.

And most of all, we want to thank the Lord Jesus Christ for commissioning us and helping us write this book and for opening doors of opportunity to see it published. May it bring Him great pleasure and glory by inspiring a generation of prayer-saturated kids!

INTRODUCTION

Natalie was manning the cash register at a newsstand in the Colorado Springs airport when I walked up to buy a magazine.

"What are you doing in Colorado Springs?" she asked.

"I've been camped out at the World Prayer Center, working on a new book. It's called *Prayer-Saturated Kids*," I replied.

"That's awesome! What's it about?"

"It's a book to help parents and spiritual leaders learn how to saturate the kids in their lives in prayer—then teach those kids how to pray for themselves. We want the next generation to be prepared to face everything that will come their way."

"That's just what we need," Natalie said. "My generation is definitely looking for guidance. Many of us weren't raised in Christian homes. We haven't had anyone to show us what this looks like. Most of us just pray when we're in trouble."

She pointed to a rack of books by Christian authors. "Is your book going to be for sale in here?"

I nodded and told her I hoped so.

"I see kids come in here all the time. They pick up those Christian books, flip through the pages, read the back cover —sometimes they even buy a copy. I think they're looking for something."

Later as I reflected upon this chance meeting with Natalie, I realized that she and others just like her are the reason we wrote *Prayer-Saturated Kids*. This book is a response to the cry of a lost generation: "Bless us, pray healing for our brokenness, and believe

God with us for our future."

I've discovered that even kids brought up in Christian homes and raised in the church lack the security of a community that builds a protective hedge around them in intercession. Somehow in the busyness of home, work, and church life, we adults miss out on opportunities to cover and train the next generation in prayer.

During the years my daughter, Nicole, was a teenager, I had the privilege of interacting with scores of Christian kids her age. They kept telling me, "We just want mothers and fathers in the faith to teach us what they know."

You may be a mom, a dad, or a pastor. You may be a prayer leader or youth or children's ministry worker. You may be a grand-parent, a schoolteacher, or a coach. No matter what your role is with kids—in whatever capacity you interact with children and teenagers—*you* are in a strategic position to equip and intercede for the next generation.

We've written this book to help you pick up the mantle of prayer leader, mentor, and prayer warrior for the children in *your* life. It will inspire you with stories of praying parents, families, communities, and churches that are raising up young people strong in faith and powerful in prayer.

Originally, a chapter called "Prayer-Saturated Kids" was supposed to be included in my book *The Prayer-Saturated Church.* After reviewing the chapter, the NavPress editorial team felt the topic was so important that it should have a book of its own. I knew at some point I would be writing *Prayer-Saturated Kids* as a follow-up to the first book. In the meantime, Arlyn Lawrence had just completed *PrayKids! Teacher's Guide: A Comprehensive Handbook for Developing Kids Who Pray* (NavPress). She was inter-ested in writing an inspirational and instructional companion to the handbook. So Arlyn and I put our heads and hearts together and wrote the book that you now hold in your hands.

Each chapter offers inspiration, instruction, and insight on a different aspect of how prayer can impact the child (or children) in your life. We've included study questions at the end of the book to make *Prayer-Saturated Kids* easily adaptable as a study course for individuals, couples, and small groups or as a curriculum supplement for homeschooling families. The Take It Out of the House section helps you apply concepts to your community. The prayer at the end of each section helps you apply in prayer what you've learned.

Key features of the book include the following:

- a child's original design — discovering and praying for God's unique plan in the life of a child
- the power of praying blessings
- healing prayers for hurting kids and families
- closing generational doors to the Enemy
- creative models and practical tools to help parents and church leaders raise up prayer-saturated children

What is a prayer-saturated kid? Quite simply, a child who is prayed for, prayed with, and taught to pray. Prayer-saturated kids are full of faith — equipped and released to pray in ways that change the world and the people around them.

I knew I was succeeding at raising a prayer-saturated kid when Nicole, at the age of thirteen, suggested to her classmates that they fast from lunch and form a prayer group to intercede for their unsaved friends. I knew the prayer power was spreading when even more prayer-saturated kids showed up at my house on Halloween night, not to trick-or-treat, but to pray for our city — all night!

Arlyn saw evidence that her elementary-age kids were prayer-saturated when their school bus driver told her she prayed over each child's assigned seat, by name, every single day before starting her route. Arlyn saw it when her teenaged son's youth pastor prayed with him and for him about deep heart concerns, an act that transformed his countenance and revitalized his relationships with his parents and with the Lord. Another mother knew she had a prayer-saturated kid when she went into her daughter's room to tell her good-night and found her fervently praying over the faces of classmates in her yearbook, picture by picture.

Many in the church agree that our nation is currently in an escalating and unprecedented prayer movement. Yet there is a deep and growing concern that this fervency for prayer—and the biblical foundations for prayer—are not being effectively passed on to the next generation. The world in which our children are growing up is increasingly uncertain, unstable, and hostile. Kids today need our prayer covering as well as equipping if they are to overcome the spiritual and practical opposition they will surely encounter in their lives.

We as parents and the church have in front of us right now the opportunity to shape the lives and destinies of the next generation. The level and quality of investment we make, through prayer, in this emerging generation will determine how effectively they will be able to navigate and succeed in what may possibly be the most intense spiritual environment in history.

Who will pass on the power of prayer to the next generation?

Who will intercede for them?

Who will teach them to hear God's voice and train them for spiritual battle?

Is it you?

— *Cheryl Sacks, 2007*

SATURATE YOUR CHILD WITH PRAYER TODAY

Father, I accept Your assignment to pray for the children You have placed in my life. Teach me how to stand guard over my own children — to pray with and for them, to leave them a legacy of prayer to pass down to their children. At the same time, make me aware of other children who will pass through the doors of my home, work, church, and community. Show me how to pray for their needs and the unspoken cry of their hearts. As I read this book, please strengthen my own prayer life, because I know I cannot give to others what I do not have myself. Give me a Spirit-filled prayer life — one that will serve as a model to the children whose lives I touch.

Father, today I commit to invest in the next generation through prayer — to plant seeds of truth, to train them, and to help pour the life of Your Spirit into them. Amen.

CHAPTER 1

A CHILD'S ORIGINAL DESIGN

You saw me before I was born.

    Every day of my life was recorded in your book.

Every moment was laid out

    before a single day had passed.

(Psalm 139:16, NLT)

"Why did they put the streets that way, Mom?"

I was getting used to questions like that from our seven-year-old son. When Tyler was quite young — younger than one would usually expect a child to be observant of such things — my husband, Doug, and I (Arlyn) noticed he had a penchant for observing and critiquing how things were laid out — things like neighborhoods, city streets, and parks.

"I would have planned those streets another way," he would say. "And why did they cut down all the trees when they built that neighborhood? I would have left a tree in every yard!"

One of the things we believe that God hardwired, so to speak, into Tyler's temperament is the quality of being a *planner*. We have not only observed this but have also sensed it strongly as we have prayed for God to show us who He designed Tyler to be. It is one of the qualities we have prayed would be developed and cultivated in Tyler's life and contribute to his living out God's unique destiny for him. We pray this way for all five of our kids. Through a combination of inquiring of the Lord, practical observation, and discernment, we have gleaned some insight into how God designed each of our children, so we can intercede—and parent—according to God's blueprint and not just our own.

Do you know how God has uniquely designed *your* child, or the children in your life? Have you looked for unique characteristics that give clues to what that design might be—personality traits, character qualities, talents, abilities, spiritual gifts, and life callings? Better yet, have you ever prayed and asked God to show you His design for your child?

You can start praying for a child's design and destiny at any age. It's never too early—or too late. Through prayer, you have the amazing opportunity and privilege to partner with God in seeing His original design for a child come to fruition as that child grows into adulthood. You can help your children become who God destined them to be. Your prayers can take the form of

- **Intercessory prayer**—praying *for* the accomplishment of God's design for a child's life, or
- **Spiritual warfare prayer**—praying *against* the schemes of the Enemy that seek to oppose, corrupt, and pervert God's original design.

Dr. Charles Boyd, in his book *Different Children, Different Needs*, says, "As parents, we need to discover our children's natural styles and help each one grow up according to his unique, inborn, God-given design." He tells a story that firmly impressed this important principle on his mind:

Some time ago I watched an episode of Beyond 2000 *on television's Discovery Channel, and I learned about a new type of metal. This "shape memory alloy," as it was called, could be programmed to "remember" a certain shape. If that original shape was distorted in some way (by twisting and bending it with your hands, for example), it could easily be restored by simply passing it through hot water. Imagine car bodies made of a metal like that—if you had a fender bender you would simply take your automobile to a nearby car wash and it would be as good as new!*[1]

"Train up a child in the way he should go," says Proverbs 22:6 (KJV), "and when he is old, he will not depart from it." Raise him or her, that is, according to the child's "natural bent." The Hebrew meaning of the phrase "in the way he should go" is literally "according to his way." The Hebrew word for "way" is *derek*, which means "bent." It refers to a unique inner design or direction, similar to the "shape memory alloy" that Dr. Boyd described. When referring to our children's natural "bents," I like to use the term "original design."

Our daughter Heather is a worshiper—expressive, sensitive, dynamic, and musically gifted. Her sister Hayley has a mother's heart—capable, practical, and organized—and loves to plan and create fun times and beautiful spaces for family and friends. Timothy and Hillary each have their own unique bents—or original design—too. Every one of God's children arrives in this world with a divinely originated design and destiny, including all the children in *your* life. As Paul noted, "For we are God's workmanship, created in Christ Jesus to do good works, *which God prepared in advance for us to do*" (Ephesians 2:10, emphasis added).

Dutch Sheets, in his book *Authority in Prayer*, says,

That God has authored a secure destiny for you can be seen in one of the New Testament words translated purpose (see

2 Timothy 1:9; Romans 8:28). It comes from the Greek word prothesis, *which means to set forth the purpose of something in advance. "Exposition" is a good meaning for it, as is thesis (a word found in the original term). God wrote His plan — an exposition, a thesis — about you before you were even born.*[2]

NOT MY WILL — BUT YOURS, LORD!

During Tyler's junior year in college he became quite anxious. It was time to declare a major, but the degree he had intended to pursue was not one he now felt comfortable with. He began to battle confusion, hopelessness, and depression.

On the home front, we felt that our primary responsibility was to pray, not to step in and fix the situation. It was hard, because we were really rather attached to his first choice of major. But we prayed that God's design and destiny would triumph in Tyler's life. We knew that God watches His Word to see that it is fulfilled (see Jeremiah 1:12). We tried to remind Ty of these truths, about what God thought of and said about him. We interceded for God's purposes to prevail.

Through a series of "coincidental" connections, Tyler received a call from the head of his university's advisory department to look at his transcripts and help him declare his major. Although discouraged by what he felt had been random choices of classes and fearful that he would consequently be in school longer than he had hoped, Ty agreed to the appointment.

When everything was laid out on the table, the adviser told him, "There's no cause for concern here. You could graduate next year with a geography degree — with a specialty in *planning.*" This particular degree would let him, if he so chose, make a career in land use and development — something for which he had had an affinity since childhood but which neither he (nor his parents) had consciously pursued! Yet it fit entirely with what we believed to be part of his original design. It was a huge confirmation from the Lord that this was the direction Tyler should pursue. Neither we nor Ty could have planned it better ourselves!

Although sometimes God does reveal His life plan for a child at an early age, we caution against making declarative statements (or prayers) that a child will be a doctor, a missionary, or a member of any other vocation. It is more helpful to recognize that a child has a heart for healing or a passion to share Christ with the world, even a heart for the nations. We can't presume exactly how God will use a child's gifts and character traits. But we can identify them and pray they be used strategically for God's purposes and according to His blueprint.

An important part of this process is releasing our own expectations and dreams of who we would like our children to be. It's all too easy to project our own hopes and desires onto them and miss entirely the plans God has for them. This can lead to conflict, disappointment, and even broken relationships between parents and children. Imagine what you will communicate to your child when you set out to discover his or her unique design and release your child to walk in it. What freedom! What a message of love, support, and encouragement! What trust in God that His will be done on earth (and in our children's lives) as it is in heaven (see Matthew 6:10)!

GOD'S DESIGN MAY SURPRISE YOU

Doug and I enrolled Tyler in soccer when he was five. For years we endured early Saturday morning games in the cold, drizzly Northwest weather. I can remember sitting there—shivering, hair dripping, my teeth chattering—watching him play and wondering why on earth I was putting myself (and him) through this.

But Doug had been somewhat of a soccer star and fan in his youth and wanted Tyler to have the same opportunity.

The year Tyler turned thirteen, his team made a move into a more demanding league and we needed to decide whether or not he would make the transition. Confident that he would want to move up with his teammates, we were shocked when, after we assured him that whatever he decided was fine with us, he declared without hesitation that he wanted nothing more to do with it! When we questioned him, he said, "I've never been crazy about soccer. You guys were always the ones who wanted me to play."

All those Saturday mornings in the rain for nothing.

At that point, we realized we were probably doing the same thing in other areas of Tyler's life. We prayerfully let him start making decisions (and changes) about other things. We also changed the way we determined what kinds of events and activities our other children should be involved in. When any of the kids came to us with a request to participate in an activity, we didn't just check the schedule and the checkbook. We began to consult the Lord, as well, asking Him if this commitment fit in with His design and plan for that child.

Sometimes His answers surprised us. When Tyler was seventeen and Heather was fifteen, our church youth group went on a Youth With A Mission trip to Mexico. Heather was torn because cheer camp was the same week, and she had just made the varsity cheer squad at her high school. We asked both Tyler and Heather to pray on their own while Doug and I each prayed about it, too. Then we would come back together and share with each other what we sensed the Lord speaking to us.

We all got the same answer. Doug and I felt strongly that the Lord was saying Tyler should go. The purpose of the trip was to build a house for an impoverished family and to do some repair and remodeling at the mission compound. This was part of what God had shown us was Tyler's individual design—industrious, skilled with his hands, a wise builder. He would learn skills and develop qualities that God would use in Tyler's life calling, whatever that would prove to be.

On the other hand, we all received in prayer that Heather was not to go, that she was to attend cheer camp instead. Frankly, this decision caused some raised eyebrows among our friends and hers. But we felt that the Lord was saying that being a cheerleader was part of His design for and calling on Heather's life—as a leader, an encourager, and a light for Jesus in her school. The experience of cheer camp would accomplish in Heather's life something similar to what the mission trip would accomplish in Tyler's. Still a mission trip—just on a different field.

Later that summer, a girlfriend from Heather's cheerleading squad came along with us on a church youth group trip, during which she gave her life to Christ. That fall, three more girls from the squad accompanied Heather and her friend to a youth outreach event, and the first two had the privilege of leading the other three to Christ!

If we had made our previous decision based on natural or reasonable criteria, we most likely would have sent both kids on the mission trip, thinking that was the more "spiritual" choice. We're glad we sought the Lord for His design and plan first—even though it surprised us at the time. It was an important step in helping us move our children toward their God-given designs and destinies.

FINDING YOUR CHILD'S PRAYER STYLE

Nine-year-old Ian was crestfallen after Sunday school one morning.

"What's wrong?" his mother, Cynthia, asked.

"They wouldn't pray for my prayer request," he said. "I wanted to pray about the panda bears in China, but they said we should pray for personal things. Why couldn't we pray about the pandas, Mom?"

Cynthia's heart sank. Ian's Sunday school teacher wasn't trying to be insensitive; she just didn't understand how God had wired Ian. From early on, Ian had had a genuine concern for what was going on in the world. When he learned that the pandas' habitat was being threatened, he was troubled.

"You know what, Ian?" Cynthia said, with new insight. "I think God is calling you to something special. He made you to notice things that other people might not understand. It *is* important to pray for the pandas in China, and for the people who make hard decisions about how to solve their country's problems. Why don't we pray for that?"

From then on, whenever Ian showed concern over something he heard in the news, Cynthia would suggest he pray about it. She realized that God had wired Ian to be an "issues intercessor," and she wanted to help develop his calling.[3]

There are different styles of prayer. And there are different styles of kids. With that in mind, be prepared for the likelihood that each child will relate to God according to God's original design and bent. We might, in this context, understand Proverbs 22:6 to say, "Train a child (*to pray*) according to his natural bent, and when he is old he will not depart from it."

When we try to force children into a cookie-cutter prayer mold, they may become so discouraged that they abandon their faith altogether because they never learned how to connect with God in a personal way. They were always just copying someone else's prayer style. Trying to imitate another person's style of praying may very well end up being a Saul's armor!

In 1 Samuel 17, we find the account of David's encounter with the Philistine giant, Goliath. In this story, King Saul urged young David to don the royal armor when he challenged Goliath.

Imagine how awkward, uncomfortable, even silly David felt as he tried to maneuver around in the ungainly stuff. Young as he was, David had the wisdom and the boldness to throw it off, saying, "I cannot go in these. . . . I am not used to them" (verse 39).

Although this passage is not specifically about prayer, it is a good analogy of what we do to our children when we fail to train them and equip them according to their original design.

An introverted, idea-oriented child, for example, may feel more comfortable expressing thoughts to God in a journal rather than praying aloud in a group (even a family group). A highly kinesthetic child who is full of energy may respond well to prayer-walking or singing. A visually oriented child may like to illustrate prayers through drawings, sculpture, or other media.

After all, even people in the Bible prayed differently! In her book *When Children Pray*, Cheri Fuller notes:

> *With prayer, there is plenty of room for individual style. When we teach children to pray — or for that matter, when we pray — it's important not to confuse style with substance, or with spirituality. Based on prayers recorded in Scripture, God responds to stylistic variations from His pray-ers. The fact that we desire to communicate with Him matters more than how we talk to Him.*
>
> *In the Bible people prayed in a variety of ways: with palms raised (Ps. 28:2), dropping to the knees (Lk. 22:41), kneeling with eyes lifted to heaven (1 Ki. 8:54), with clapping, dancing, and singing (Acts 16:25). There were shouted prayers (Josh. 6:16-20), and prayers without words (1 Sam. 22:2-3). The stylistic differences were both creative and indicative of each pray-er's personality, mood, and requests.*[4]

Now, that's not to say that we don't teach our children a variety of expressions of prayer. But we do need to be sensitive to the fact that some modes of communication with God may be more comfortable and effective for each child than others, according to how He has designed that child. See how throughout Scripture God demonstrates His involvement in the blueprint for a child's life. Let these passages build your faith to pray for the original design God has for children in your life, whether they be your own or others that He puts in your path:

- God told Jeremiah (as an adult), "Before I formed you in the womb I knew you, before you were born I set you apart; I appointed you as a prophet to the nations" (Jeremiah 1:5).
- Rebekah specifically inquired of the Lord about the twin babies in her womb, and God answered her. The Lord said to her, "Two nations are in your womb, and two peoples from within you will be separated; one people will be stronger than the other, and the older will serve the younger" (Genesis 25:23).
- The angel of the Lord told Samson's mother even before she became pregnant, "You are sterile and childless, but you are going to conceive and have a son. Now see to it that you drink no wine or other fermented drink and that you do not eat anything unclean, because you will conceive and give birth to a son. No razor may be used on his head, because the boy is to be a Nazirite, set apart to God from birth, and he will begin the deliverance of Israel from the hands of the Philistines" (Judges 13:3-5).
- An angel appeared to Zacharias, father of John the Baptist, to give him insight into his son's destiny—before the child was even conceived! "He will be great in the sight of the Lord" (Luke 1:15).
- An angel appeared to Joseph in a dream to reveal God's

destiny for the child his fiancée was carrying: "What is conceived in her is from the Holy Spirit. She will give birth to a son, and you are to give him the name Jesus, because he will save his people from their sins" (Matthew 1:20-21).

- An angel gave similar insight about Jesus to Mary: "He will be great and will be called the Son of the Most High. The Lord God will give him the throne of his father David, and he will reign over the house of Jacob forever; his kingdom will never end" (Luke 1:32-33).

PRAYING FOR YOUR CHILD'S ORIGINAL DESIGN

In what ways has God designed your children differently from others—or from you? Original design shows up in a variety of ways. It can manifest itself in a child's

- **Temperament**—Is he or she fast-paced or slow-paced? People-oriented or task-oriented? Introverted or extroverted? Intense or easy going?
- **Talents and aptitudes**—Is he or she musical? Mechanical? Mathematical? Linguistic? Artistic?
- **Spiritual gifts**—If a believer, does he or she demonstrate gifts of mercy? Leadership? Encouragement? Exhortation? Prophecy? Wisdom? Discernment?
- **Calling**—Perhaps he or she is called to be a communicator, a shepherd, a teacher, a leader, a mother or father, a worshiper, a manager, or a warrior.
- **Capacity**—Has he been assigned a large sphere of influence, or a small one? Is she a multitasker, or single-focused? Can he handle large amounts of detail and input

at once, or does he need to receive instructions one or two at a time with time to process?

You will find clues to your children's original design in their behavior, their likes and dislikes, the kinds of friends they choose, the kinds of games they play, and so on. Become a student of your children. Find out what makes them tick.

Gary Smalley and John Trent in their book *The Blessing* note that "Children are filled with the potential to be all God intended them to be."[5] They give some insightful questions you can ask to learn more about whom God designed your children to be and how He has uniquely wired them to accomplish His purposes for their lives:

1. What do they most often dream about?
2. When they think of their years as a young adult (twenty to thirty), what would they really enjoy doing?
3. Of all the people they have studied in the Bible, who is the person they would most like to be like, and why?
4. What do they believe God wants them to do for humankind?
5. [for older children] What type of boyfriend or girlfriend are they most interested in, and why?
6. What is the best part of their school day, and what is the worst?[6]

You can also listen to God's voice telling you how He made your children. The Holy Spirit may show you specific character qualities as you pray and listen for His voice. Or, long after you've actually prayed about it, He may give you a flash of divine insight when you least expect it. Listen, take note, and meditate on what the Lord reveals, even as Mary meditated on the things the angel revealed to her about Jesus: "But Mary treasured up all these things and pondered them in her heart" (Luke 2:19).

TAKE IT OUT OF THE HOUSE

Church nursery ministers and children's leaders can pray to see God's design for the children in their ministries. When you're rocking the babies, changing their diapers, or soothing their cries, pray words of life and destiny over them. Ask the Lord to show you whom He designed them to be.

I remember once trying to comfort ten-month-old Brooke in the nursery so her mother could lead a women's small group. The more I rocked, the louder she wailed! I asked the Lord to show me who this tough little cookie might grow up to be and then began to speak back to her what I sensed in my spirit. "Brookie, you are a strong woman. You will be a great leader for God's kingdom someday. You will be a bright light for Jesus. You will stand firm against the Enemy's schemes." Then I turned these statements into prayers on Brooke's behalf. Later, I shared them with her mom.

For older children, be observant and prayerful in your interactions with them. Listen to what they talk about. Observe their actions. Are they encouragers? Leaders? Ask the Lord to point out to you clues to their original design. During ministry times, speak those words of purpose and destiny into them. Remember to pray for these young people throughout the week. Pray that God's original design for them will be cultivated and advanced in their lives.

In my daughter Hillary's Sunday school class, the children's ministry team talked and prayed with the children about components of each child's original design. They noted qualities like "encourager," "prayer warrior," "gentle spirit," "leader," and "compassionate friend." They had kids write these words on construction paper, then glue photos on, too. The teachers hung these on the classroom wall as a constant reminder of how God sees those kids.

SATURATE YOUR CHILD WITH PRAYER TODAY

Lord, I thank You that You knew _____
*in the womb, and even sooner, and You designed and declared
a marvelous plan for this child's life. I want to be able to see
this child the way You do, Lord. Please point out to me the
unique characteristics You have woven into* _____*'s
temperament. Give me insight into* _____*'s calling
and destiny. Help me to encourage and pray for* _____
*according to the natural bent that You planned — close to You,
led by You, and fulfilling Your original design in every area
of this child's life. Amen.*

CHAPTER 2

MAKING YOUR HOME A HOUSE OF PRAYER

He who fears the LORD has a secure fortress,
and for his children it will be a refuge.
(Proverbs 14:26)

We couldn't seem to make a decision.

Doug and I (Arlyn) were thinking about selling our house and moving to another community. We had sought prayer from friends and from one of our pastors and his wife, and all had confirmed the same answer. Still, we felt unsettled and unable to move forward.

Finally, we asked our children to pray with us about it. We held an emergency family meeting then, after briefly discussing the subject (which was understandably emotionally charged), we went straight to prayer. We asked the Lord to speak to all of us, and then asked everyone to share what he or she felt the Lord was saying to us.

As we prayed, the pieces of the puzzle seemed to fall into place and we felt a sense of peace we hadn't felt up to this point. Finally, we were in unity. We all even began to feel a sense of excitement as we anticipated our family's future in a new community.

One of the mottoes in our household is "Worry about nothing; pray about everything!" That's our rendition of Philippians 4:6. We try to make prayer our rule of thumb, whether it's about missing keys, an illness, a troubled relationship, or a disobedient child. Our daughter Hayley once rolled her eyes and exclaimed with exasperation, "Oh Mom, you pray about *everything!*"

BUILDING A HOUSE OF PRAYER

When our house was being built, Doug crawled beneath the front deck to get under the frame of the front door. There, just above the foundation, he wrote the following paraphrased passage: "The LORD our God, the LORD is one. We will love the Lord our God with all our heart and with all our soul and with all our strength" (see Deuteronomy 6:4-5). On a long piece of wood that he screwed into place just under the front step—clearly visible to all—he inscribed Joshua 24:15, KJV: "As for me and my house, we will serve the Lord." Anyone coming in and out of our home—including all of us on a daily basis—would have to cross over the words of these Scriptures.

We were taking seriously the rest of the Deuteronomy 6 passage: "These commandments that I give you today are to be upon your hearts. Impress them on your children. . . . *Write them on the doorframes of your houses and on your gates.*" (verses 6-9, emphasis added). We had our children write Scripture promises on the unfinished doorframes of their bedrooms and dedicate them to the Lord. Before we moved in, we gathered friends and family for a prayer of dedication. We wanted our new home to be a sanctuary of God's presence and protection—and more than anything, we wanted it to be a house of prayer.

In her book *The Praying Family*, Kim Butts describes how when she and her family move to a new home, they dedicate it to the Lord. They anoint the doorpost of each door (inside and out), claiming it for Christ and His purposes. They consecrate (set apart) their house for His use and pray that He will use their home to bring many people to Himself. Kim notes that you never really know what may have gone on in your home before it was yours, so this is also a good way to serve notice to the Enemy that he cannot hang around![1]

Have you ever dedicated your house to God? You don't have to wait until you buy or build a new home to dedicate it to the Lord; you can do it any time. You may not even live in a house — you can dedicate an apartment, a motor home, or even a single room.

THE FOUNDATION: PRAYING PARENTS

One of the best gifts parents can give their children is the gift of a good marriage — knit together through prayer. It's been said that the family that prays together, stays together — but do you know just how true that is? A 1993 Gallup poll revealed that among married couples who attend church together regularly, the divorce rate is one out of two. That's the same statistic as for marriages outside the church. However, among couples who pray together daily, the divorce rate is one out of 1,153.[2] What a difference!

Prayer builds unity and intimacy. We become intimate *to whom* we pray, *for whom* we pray, and *with whom* we pray. Prayer is the key to unlocking extraordinary blessings for children and families the way a key unlocks a gate.

A few years ago, Scott and Kelly became deeply disturbed when they noticed a change for the worse in their teenage son, Caleb. Since getting involved in heavy metal rock music, Caleb had become depressed, withdrawn, and sullen. He spent hours in his room with the door closed listening to CDs of heavy metal rock as well as playing the music on his guitar. At night he often had terrible dreams and attacks of fear and panic. Previously, Caleb had been a good student and committed to prayer, Bible reading, and church.

Scott and Kelly tried to talk to Caleb and get him to open up, but the more they tried the further Caleb pulled away. They decided they would commit to pray especially and intentionally for Caleb every day. And at the same time, Scott, out of pure desperation, began to slip into Caleb's room each night—after Caleb was fast asleep—to pray. Each night Scott would stretch himself out on the carpet beside Caleb's bed—as he quietly cried out for the Lord to deliver his son.

One Saturday about three weeks later, Scott and Kelly heard a commotion in the garage—sounds of crashing and breaking and someone crying and intermittently screaming and sobbing. They ran to the garage and found Caleb, tears rolling down his face and hammer in hand as he over and over again pounded into bits his large pile of metal rock music CDs.

These parents knew their role as gatekeepers—closing the door of their home to the Enemy and opening the door to Christ's healing through prayer.

A MOTHER'S WATCHFUL PRAYERS

It may appear to a child that Mom has "eyes in the back of her head," but that may seem especially true if she's a *praying* mom! Proverbs 31:27 says, "She *watches* over the affairs of her household" (emphasis added). God appoints a mom to watch over her family, I believe, the way He appoints a watchman to watch over a city (see Isaiah 62:6). The words *watches* and *watchman* in Scripture have similar meanings: "to peer into the distance, observe, watch; to hedge about (as with thorns), guard, protect, attend to."[3] They can also be translated "lookout" or "doorkeeper."[4] Some people like to use the word "intercessor" or "prayer warrior." Intercession is one of the most powerful tasks a mother can undertake. Much more can be accomplished for our children from our knees than from our mouths.

One mom, Eleanor, found this out when her thirteen-year-old adopted son, Eugene, had not grown even an eighth of an inch in a year. At first she thought it was just his Asian heritage; then her doctor told her to take him to a specialist who would prescribe growth hormones. But during one of her times with God, He showed her a specific Scripture verse she could pray for her son. She paraphrased it: "Lord, may my son, like Jesus, increase in wisdom and stature and favor with God and man" (see Luke 2:52).

In the first three months after she started praying this way, Eugene grew three inches—without hormone shots! In the next three months, he grew three more. His conduct grade on his report card went from a C- to an A. "Mom," he said, "my teacher likes me now, and I like her." Eugene increased in stature and favor with this teacher and also in wisdom, as his other grades improved as well.[5]

Well-known pastor E. V. Hill shares the benefits of a praying mom in his own life:

> *I came from a broken family. My mother's income was twelve dollars a week. We had no welfare, we had no Aid to Dependent Children; we didn't have nothing but what we made during the summer by picking cotton and shaking peanuts. Five of us lived out in the country in a two-room log cabin. We didn't have much, but we knew how to pray. Mama left me nothing that required a will, but she taught me how to pray at an early age. When there was no money for a doctor and no white doctors would see us in my county, my mama laid her hands on me and prayed. When there was no hope that I should finish high school my mama said, "God gonna send you through high*

school." *And when I finished high school, my mama shocked the whole community by saying, "Ed's going to college," and I did. I am the result of my mother's prayers.*[6]

THE STRATEGIC ROLE OF PRAYING DADS

Kids need to hear their dads praying for them! Even though some men may feel their wives pray with their children more naturally than they do (women tend to be more verbal), they shouldn't let that stop them. Cheryl relates that

> *when Nicole was a little girl, Hal was often away on mission trips. During these times, especially at night, Nicole felt unsettled. She missed her dad and the sense of safety he brought to our home. On several occasions Nicole lay awake all night crying. The next morning she was so worn out she would have to stay home from preschool. So when Hal discovered he would be taking a two-week trip to the Philippines, we were concerned about how this was going to affect Nicole.*
>
> *One night just before the trip, Hal went into Nicole's room and sat down on her bed. He talked about God's protection and the work of guardian angels. Then he prayed over her and read the Scripture from Psalm 91:11, AMP: "He will give His angels [especial] charge over you to accompany and defend and preserve you in all your ways."*
>
> *The following morning after Hal left for the Philippines, Nicole awoke and told me what had happened during the night. "The angels came last night, Mommy!" she exclaimed. "They were standing in a circle around my bed, singing. It was the most beautiful singing I've ever heard!"*
>
> *"What did they look like?" I questioned.*
>
> *"Some were so tall their heads touched the ceiling and*

some were little like me. Some had on gold sandals, and some had on gold belts. And they were so white—the whitest white I've ever seen!"

I might have been tempted to dismiss Nicole's experience as childish imagination, had I not had a similar experience some fifteen years earlier. At a time in my life when I felt frightened and all alone, I awoke to find a huge angel standing over me. He was so tall his head touched the ceiling and his wings were the whitest white I'd ever seen! The light was so bright I couldn't keep my eyes open! The presence of the Lord permeated my being and I felt a powerful sense of God's peace and protection.

Nicole never again cried about her dad being away or mentioned being fearful because of his absence. When Hal exercised his authority in prayer, he shut fear out of our home and invited the protection and presence of God to dwell there.

Doug shares how he learned something similar in the Lawrence household:

Early in my married life, I began to realize my personal responsibility for the spiritual well-being of my wife and children—that my leadership (or sometimes lack of it) deeply affected what transpired spiritually under our roof. I could not accomplish spiritual work in my family through edicts or religious activities, but I could through my prayers. And when I took the initiative to begin praying—on my own, with my wife, with my children, and for them all—many things began to change. I found, to my surprise, that my prayer life did not have to look like that of my wife—or anyone else, for that matter. It just simply had to be a work between God and me—one that I took seriously. I soon discovered that prayer was much more effective as a first response than as a last resort.

WHEN YOU GET UP: MORNING PRAYERS

It's tempting to rush right out the door in the morning without taking the time to sit down, invite God into your family's life, and give the events of your children's day to Him. But morning prayers don't need to be a long, drawn-out affair. They can be as simple as an acknowledgment of His presence and a request for His protection and provision throughout the day.

Your kids may have some specific concerns—even fears—about events that may transpire that day. Praying with them in the morning can help alleviate that kind of anxiety and give an opportunity for them to see God working in their lives at a very intimate, personal level. Even if you don't stop for a formal prayer time, a great way to send everyone out of the house in the morning is with a prayer of blessing (see chapter 3). A daily blessing imparts God's presence into the lives of our children in a way that makes them feel loved—by God and by us!

WHEN YOU ARE AT HOME: MEALTIME PRAYERS

In our own busy family, dinnertime has always been the one time we are pretty much guaranteed to all be in the same place at the same time. With seven work, school, sports, and church ministry schedules, we're rarely all in the same room together—except at dinnertime. So that's when we have our most regular family prayer time.

Perhaps you want to choose to make dinnertime a regular family prayer time. To avoid loud eruptions of "Hurry up, the food's getting cold!" I offer the following suggestions:

1. Have only one (or no more than two) family members pray before the meal. Each night a different person can pray.
2. Let thanksgiving to God for the food (and the hands that prepared it) be the primary theme. When our family prays together in a restaurant, we ask God to bless the chefs and servers, too.
3. Offer a prayer of intercession for someone everyone in the family knows, such as an extended family member, a neighbor, a friend, your pastor, or a missionary from your church.
4. As an alternative to intercession, offer a prayer of petition (request) for a need the whole family is aware of, such as a financial or health concern, a lost pet, a new job, a passing grade on a test, or whatever the Lord brings to mind.
5. Close with a declaration of faith in God: "God, You're awesome! We know You hear and we thank You for that. Thanks that we can talk to You! We pray in the powerful name of Jesus. Amen." Let your children know that *amen* means "so be it" and is actually an affirmation of faith and agreement.

WHEN YOU LIE DOWN: BEDTIME PRAYERS

Children love to be "tucked in" at night. This is one of the best times to turn a child's heart to the Lord in prayer. As your child opens up about the events of the day and maybe even begins to confide in you, suggest, "Let's talk to the Lord about that." Your child will be assured that you're listening and that you consider what he or she said to be important. Your child will feel secure when he or she hears you taking the need, concern, or request to an even higher authority.

Nighttime prayers are also a great opportunity to affirm what your child prays. I love the story of how three-year-old Michaela looked around her room during her bedtime prayer and thanked God for everything she could see—including her curtains and her Barbie dolls. Her mother could have discouraged her, saying, "Honey, let's find some new things to pray about—I don't think God really cares very much about every little thing in your room." Instead, her mother wisely said, "Honey, that was a great prayer! I'm sure God is so pleased that you are such a thankful little girl! Let's spend a little bit of time praying for our family tonight, too, okay?" She then proceeded to pray for other family members, which Michaela picked up on quickly and joined in.

This mother did two important things: She recognized the validity and importance of her little one's prayer before God, and she modeled a way for her child to stretch and grow in prayer.[7]

WHEN YOU WALK ALONG THE WAY: PRAYING THROUGH THE CHALLENGES OF FAMILY LIFE

Being a house of prayer means that prayer is the rule of thumb for every need, concern, challenge, or opportunity. When our youngest daughter, Hillary, was five, she was suddenly struck with a high fever in the middle of the night. I had no children's pain reliever on hand, so Doug and I made a bed for her on the floor of our room, placed cool cloths on her forehead, and settled down to (hopefully) get back to sleep. A few minutes later, a plaintive voice came up from the floor.

"I just need someone to *pray* for me!"

Doug, somewhat sheepish that he hadn't thought of it first, reached down and instructed Hillary to grasp his hand in the dark. He rebuked the fever the way Jesus did for Peter's mother-in-law in Luke 4:39: "In Jesus' name, I command this fever to leave!" Then he prayed for the peace and healing of God's Spirit to cover her and give her rest.

Content, Hillary drifted off to sleep. In the morning, she was perfectly healthy and even more convinced of the power of prayer — as were her parents!

When the issues are not heavy, children can be involved in most of the kinds of prayer that adults can. This is the best way to not only model prayer, but also to build faith that will last a lifetime.

Gail was at a loss for how to include her three girls in her husband's talent management company, which he was operating out of their home. She told her friend Bobbie, wife of her husband's business partner, that she wanted to find a way for the children to feel a part of the business. Bobbie's idea was to match up people who were part of the business with Gail's girls as prayer partners. She helped the girls make prayer journals, which they created by pasting pictures from cards and adding their own artwork. The journals included pages for thanksgiving, praise, God's promises, and requests.

Each girl chose pictures of a staff person and one client she would pray for. One Wednesday, four-year-old Marissa received an SOS call that Mr. Martin's computer was frozen. It was naptime, but she grabbed her prayer journal so she could pray before she fell asleep. Marissa couldn't wait to tell Mr. Martin that she had prayed for him. The best news was his reply: "Thanks, Marissa. I had the best sales of the entire month that day."[8]

Another mom, Stacy, experienced a particularly challenging week. The family's business had recently failed, and her husband was on the road as a salesman. At home with their five children, Stacy realized there was no money left and only a few groceries in the house. As these supplies dwindled with each meal, she remembered God's faithfulness. Stacy prayed that God would bless their provisions, multiplying them to last as long as necessary. At the end of the week, their last meal of the day finally brought an end to the food. As usual, Stacy and the children prayed together at bedtime. She reminded them of Philippians 4:19: "And my God will meet all your needs according to his glorious riches in Christ Jesus."

After tucking the children in bed, Stacy went downstairs and sat in her "prayer chair." The ringing telephone startled her. The caller said, "I've been feeling like you could really use some help right now; I just sent $150 to you, and it should be there in the morning."[9]

Do you have similar stories of God's intervention in your life? You can reinforce the thrill of answered prayer for your children by providing ways to record what God has done. Keep a prayer journal in which you jot down the times and ways that your family's prayers are answered. Or make a "jar of remembrance" in which you place stones with answered prayers recorded on them, written in permanent ink. Over the years, you may just acquire a large collection of stone-filled jars!

YOUR HOME AS A PRAYER REST STOP

When Cheryl's niece Brooke was young, Cheryl enjoyed having her come for special visits. Together they would talk, visit, and catch up on each other's lives. On one particular visit, Cheryl pulled out craft supplies and helped Brooke make a prayer journal as a tool to help her continue at home what she had done with her aunt — a special memento of their time together that would hopefully help create a lasting legacy of prayer in Brooke's life.

Many children and families pass through our homes on a regular basis, from relatives to neighbors to classmates. Being a house of prayer means that our homes can function as kind of a "prayer rest stop" for these people, the way a roadside rest stop provides refreshment and resources to travelers on our nation's freeways.

When we met our new neighbors, Sean and Kristin, Kristin was working full time and had no after-school child care for her two girls. I volunteered to keep the girls each day after they got off the school bus, until she came home from work. One day when Kristin came to pick the girls up, she was nearly fainting from a terrible migraine headache. I had an impression that this was a spiritual attack as much as a physical one, so I sat her down, laid my hands on her head, and prayed for God's healing to flow into her body and any schemes of the Enemy against her to be broken, in Jesus' name. Within minutes her pain and dizziness faded. God's power had been clearly demonstrated in an undeniable way! Just a few weeks later, Kristin received Christ as her Savior, as did both of the girls.

LEAVING A LEGACY OF PRAYER

It's natural to want to leave a legacy to our children and grand-children. Some people try to do this by leaving them large sums of money. Others establish endowments, prestigious reputations, investment portfolios, or real estate holdings. While these things may give provision in a material sense for a limited time, only prayer can pay dividends that last for eternity.

When George McLuskey married and started a family, he decided to pray one hour a day for his kids to follow Christ. After a time, he expanded his prayers to include his grandchildren and great-grandchildren. Every day between 11 a.m. and noon, he prayed for the next three generations.

As the years went by, his two daughters committed their lives to Christ and married men who went into full-time ministry. The two couples produced four girls and one boy. Each of the girls married a minister, and the boy became a pastor. The first two children born to this generation were both boys. Upon graduation from high school, the two cousins chose the same college and became room-mates. During their sophomore year, one boy decided to go into the ministry. The other didn't. He undoubtedly felt some pressure to continue the family legacy, but he chose instead to pursue his interest in psychology. He earned a doctorate and eventually wrote books for parents, titles that became best sellers. He started a radio program heard on more than a thousand stations each day. The man's name—James Dobson.[10]

We can be part of a lasting legacy to future generations by filling our homes with prayer and partnering with God in helping the children in our lives find and fulfill their God-given destinies!

TAKE IT OUT OF THE HOUSE

Churches can (and should) be dedicated in the same way that we can consecrate our homes to the Lord—and children can be a part of this, too. When some of our church's adult prayer teams were praying through our new church building, doing spiritual housecleaning and prayers of dedication, I (Arlyn) took a group of fourteen children, ages one through eleven, on a prayerwalk to do a little dedication of their own.

I read them the account in Scripture of how God promised the Israelites that everywhere the soles of their feet stepped, He was giving into their hands (see Joshua 1:3; 10:8). We talked about what that might look like for our church family, in light of our being in a new church building and a new neighborhood. We talked about how God wanted to use our prayers to make this new church building a refuge and a lighthouse for everyone who would come there.

To put our prayers into action, we traced the children's hands and feet onto construction paper and cut out multiple copies. We placed the footprints on the ground around the outside of the building, and the handprints on the doors and walls, to emphasize God's promise that everywhere we placed the soles of our feet He would give to us.

With the baby perched on my hip and a teenager to help me herd the rest of the kids, we marched around the building and prayed aloud, placing our feet on the footprints and hands on the handprints.

Those kids prayed heartfelt prayers of dedication for their new church building, that it would be a house of prayer for all peoples—a lighthouse that would draw families and individuals into new life in Jesus and restore them to their heavenly Father.

SATURATE YOUR CHILD WITH PRAYER TODAY

Dear God, I dedicate my home to You. I pray that You will fill it with Your presence and truly make it a "house of prayer." I dedicate myself to You, that You will make me a strong prayer leader in the life of my child (or children). I dedicate my child (or children) to you and ask You to speak to them—and them to You—in ways that will profoundly influence the course of their lives. I determine that in this house, prayer will always be the first response instead of a last resort. Help me minister to the people who enter my home the way You would, Lord—so their hearts will be transformed by Your love and power. Amen.

CHAPTER 3

THE POWER OF
BLESSING

One day some parents brought their children to
Jesus so he could lay his hands on them and pray for
them. . . . Jesus said, "Let the children come to me.
Don't stop them! For the Kingdom of Heaven belongs
to those who are like these children." And he placed
his hands on their heads and blessed them. (Matthew
19:13-15, NLT)

"O Lord, help Hal manage his time wisely today, and please help
Nicole stop fighting me about taking naps!"

Those were good prayers. I (Cheryl) was sincere in what I had
asked. Yet I felt I wanted to go deeper. At this point in my life I
had not yet discovered one of the most powerful ways of interceding for my family—the life-giving spiritual release of imparting
blessings!

That all changed early one morning as I paced my living room
floor, lifting requests to the Lord for my husband, Hal, and four-
year-old daughter, Nicole. I wanted to pray more of God's heart for
my family and told the Lord so. As I continued, my petitions to God
suddenly began to change, turning into declarations of blessing.

"I bless Hal with wisdom, knowledge, and understanding in every decision he will face today," I heard myself quoting from Colossians 1:9. "I bless him with a faithful heart as my husband and with the ability to be a loving, caring, involved father to Nicole. I bless him with favor and influence to sit among the elders of the gates of our city," flowed the words from Proverbs 31.

With renewed excitement, my attention turned to my daughter. "In Jesus' name I bless Nicole with peace and joy that springs up like a bubbling fountain. I bless her with faith, hope, and love—with good health (physically, mentally, and emotionally). I bless Nicole with protection—may Your guardian angels defend and watch over her. I bless her with healthy friendships and in the future with Your perfect choice of a mate. I bless her with a sensitive spirit, a tender conscience, and a heart that runs hard after You all the days of her life."

Suddenly it was as if heaven itself had come down into my living room. I sensed the Lord directing my prayers in a fresh way. It seemed His face was shining upon me—that He, rather than I, was orchestrating the prayer time.

This should have come as no surprise because, after all, blessing is God's idea. He was the first to bless His children in Genesis 1: "God blessed them and said to them, 'Be fruitful and increase in number; fill the earth and subdue it'" (verse 28).

Since that morning Hal and I have continued to bless Nicole along her life's journey. We wrapped our arms around her and blessed her as she went off to kindergarten, on numerous birthdays, when she left home to work in youth ministry, and on her wedding day.

As we've grown in our understanding of this powerful principle, we also have blessed other kids of all ages whom God has brought into our lives—all our young relatives, my English students, the kids who live next door, and several hundred teenagers flowing through our home and in church settings. Sometimes we prayed while the kids were in our presence, and at other times we prayed for those who had no knowledge of what we were doing. Either way, praying blessings for a young person is like giving him a tangible present that he will be unwrapping for the rest of his life.

Today, it seems that the concept of praying blessings over the next generation has been forgotten. However, Old Testament saints understood the power of blessing. Abraham blessed Isaac, and Isaac blessed Jacob. Jacob blessed his twelve sons. These blessings were not just empty prayers or flowery words. As we read through the Bible we discover that the blessings people prayed actually came to pass.

GIVING THE BLESSING

A number of years ago, Randy and Lisa Wilson discovered that the principle of blessing runs all throughout God's Word. They tell their story in their video *Daddy's Blessing*. One afternoon Randy and Lisa gathered their children (all preschoolers at the time) in the living room and held a blessing ceremony. Randy admits that he was a little nervous and felt awkward at first, yet he didn't let this stop him. He told the children individually how special they were to their parents and to God, then he blessed each one with destiny and divine purpose.

The children are all teenagers now and the blessing ceremonies have become weekly events. One by one the children kneel in front of Randy to receive the blessing.

"You are a mighty man of God, a warrior, a child of the King," Randy tells his son Colten. "Your name means 'man of honor,' " he speaks over Logan.

To his daughter Jordon, "You reflect the essence of God's beauty. Your very name means victorious one; you are that in this world," he tells Lauren.

"You are beautiful, a princess," he speaks over Khrystian. "God will use you to influence the generations to come as you are obedient to Him." "Kameryn, your name means 'beloved, sweetheart.' You will be a great blessing to all your relationships and draw many to God's kingdom."[1]

As Gary Smalley and John Trent explain in their book *The Blessing*, every child is looking for a blessing from his or her parents. Many seek this blessing their whole lives — often in all the wrong places — never seeming to find it. Even if your own parents didn't give you the blessing you were looking for, you can pass on this gift to the children in your life. A blessing carries with it affirmation, encouragement, favor, and hope for the future. Giving a blessing places high value upon the person receiving it. A blessing may have several parts.

Closeness and Meaningful Touch. We can pray blessings over our children when they don't know we are praying for them — such as every day while they're in school, when they're grown up and living in another city, or even when they are estranged from us. Yet praying blessings when you can look into a child's eyes, say, "I love you," and give a hug is especially meaningful. At times, laying hands on a young person's head or shoulders may be more appropriate, especially when you are praying for older children and others God brings into your life such as students, neighbors, and kids from the church youth group. Jesus said, "Let the little children come to me, and do not hinder them, for the kingdom of God belongs to such as these." Then, "he took the children in his arms, put his hands on them and blessed them" (Mark 10:13-14,16).

Spoken Words of High Value. Imparting a parental blessing begins with a spoken prayer that affirms the high value that both the parent and the Lord place upon the child. You may want to begin by thanking God for the blessing the child has been in your own life. Examples of this might include expressing appreciation for a sweet spirit, truthfulness, loyalty, helpfulness, or a good sense of humor. When we bless a child, it's essential that the child instantly recognizes the words of our prayer as something valuable and beneficial in his or her life. It may be tempting for us parents to turn a blessing for our children into a mini-sermon or subtle correction. Yet a true blessing conveys a genuine desire for God to enrich a child's life.

Asking God's Blessing for a Special Future. An important part of the blessing is helping your child picture a future full of blessing. Create a vision for the future that lifts hope and builds faith. Each blessing should convey a sense that your child is anointed or chosen by God for a special purpose.[2]

Your prayer might go something like this: "Father, I thank You that You have a plan for Jason's life. Thank You for the gift You have given him to help his sisters settle arguments. Thank You that he is a peacemaker. I bless Jason with the wisdom to know how to use all his gifts for You. Open his eyes to see the wonderful future You have planned for him."

God paints a picture of how He sees our children's future through the prophet Jeremiah: "'For I know the plans I have for you,' says the LORD. 'They are plans for good and not for disaster, to give you a future and a hope'" (29:11, NLT). Most Old Testament blessings begin with "May the Lord bless you with/by . . ." This is an act of calling upon God's favor and gifts to help bring our child or another we are praying for into his or her God-given destiny.

If you're unsure about where or how to start blessing the child in your life, why not let a special event mark the time? This could include the birth of a child or grandchild, entering the teen years (much like the Jewish tradition of the bar and bat mitzvahs), leaving home, or going off to college.

One day in her morning prayer time, my friend Mary Ruth Swope was musing over the fact that she lived so far away from her daughter's only child, Daniel. It saddened her to think she would not have the opportunity to influence his spiritual, social, emotional, and physical development the way her own maternal grandmother had influenced her. As she prayed about her dilemma, Mary Ruth began to think about how in Jewish culture parents regularly bless their children:

> *I thought, "Why couldn't I begin to bless my grandson every time I speak to him on the telephone? That would be a way to transfer my personal and spiritual values to Daniel when I cannot be physically present with him."*
>
> *Immediately I began to write blessings. The next time I phoned Daniel, I told him I wanted to bless him. He listened intently and then responded sweetly, "Thank you, Grandmother."*
>
> *Four days later, I gave him a second blessing. The third time I called, I was ready to say good-bye when he asked, "Grandmother, are you going to bless me today?"*
>
> *My heart almost leapt out of my chest as I realized God was confirming to me how meaningful the blessings had been to my precious grandson.*
>
> *Now, on a regular basis, I bless Daniel over the phone, focusing on a different area of his body, personality, or spiritual, physical, and emotional needs. I now feel closer to him than ever before.*[3]

THE POWER BEHIND THE BLESSING

In his book *The Power of Spoken Blessings*, Bill Gothard says that three innate powers cause a spoken blessing to be so effective: the power of our words, the power of God's Word, and the power of the Lord's name.[4]

The power of our words. Scripture tells us, "Death and life are in the power of the tongue" (Proverbs 18:21, ESV). Words are containers of spirit. With them we can produce devastating damage or release life-giving virtue. Many other Scriptures in Proverbs reference the tongue: "The tongue of the wise brings healing" (12:18, ESV) and "Timely advice is lovely, like golden apples in a silver basket" (25:11, NLT).

The power of God's Word. Though God's work of speaking the world into existence was completed in six days, His powerful Word is still creating today (see Hebrews 4:12). When our words are combined with God's Word in a verbal blessing, we become a channel through which God's power can flow. A lightning rod provides a path for lightning and guides it to the ground. In the same way, our prayers of blessing over our children can serve as points of attraction for the power of God to flow in and through their lives.

The power of the Lord's name. In Numbers 6:23-27, God gave precise words for how the priests were to communicate a spoken blessing:

> *"Tell Aaron and his sons to bless the people of Israel with this special blessing:*
>
> > *'May the LORD bless you*
> > *and protect you.*
> > *May the LORD smile on you*
> > *and be gracious to you.*
> > *May the LORD show you his favor*
> > *and give you his peace.'*
>
> > *Whenever Aaron and his sons bless the people of Israel in my name, I myself will bless them." (NLT)*

To invoke the name of God is to call upon His power to carry out the blessing. A blessing gives life, and life is in the power of the name of the Lord.

ARE YOUR WORDS A BLESSING OR A CURSE?

Our words are containers that carry either creative or destructive power toward the people in our lives, including children. Your mouth is a weapon—either for Satan or against him. Two powerful forces are simultaneously at work in this world—blessing and cursing. These two words occur more than 640 times in the Bible. God designed our tongues to be fountains of blessing, releasing His love, His power, His healing, and His grace on the people around us. In contrast to a blessing, which *empowers to prosper*, a curse, quite simply, means to *cause to fail*. Sadly, all too often the people in our lives whom we love the most—those we want to see God bless, protect, and prosper more than anyone else—are the ones we unwittingly curse.

You may be saying, "Well, *curse* is a pretty strong word. I would never curse anyone, especially my children." However, *curse* is the word the Bible uses to describe the vocabulary of a person who does not control his speech:

> *How great a forest is set ablaze by such a small fire! And the tongue is a fire, a world of unrighteousness. The tongue is set among our members, staining the whole body, setting on fire the entire course of life, and set on fire by hell. . . . With it we bless our Lord and Father, and with it we curse people who are made in the likeness of God. From the same mouth come blessing and cursing. My brothers, these things ought not to be so. (James 3:5-6,9-10, ESV)*

A few words spoken in wrath or frustration can change the destiny of a child. Words that vibrate in the air only a few seconds can reverberate in a life as long as it lasts. Negative, hurtful words can break a child's spirit and do great damage to self-esteem as well as hurt your relationship with the child.

Ralph was a victim of verbal abuse as he grew up. Ralph's self-worth was devastated, and his ability to function was greatly damaged. He feared being around his father and closed off his spirit toward him. This was Ralph's way of saying, "You have hurt me, and I am going to make you sorry for what you have done. I am going to cut you off so that you can't hurt me any more."

Ralph's response to his father was quite normal and logical.[5] Ephesians 6:4 encourages fathers not to irritate and provoke their children to anger—not to break their spirits. Children need to be disciplined and corrected, of course, yet parents would be wise to choose their words carefully during times of stress with their children.

Angry words that convey to a child that he or she is useless or stupid can cause deep wounds that produce problems well into adulthood. While we might tell our children that their behavior is bad, it's important to reinforce that they themselves have the ability, through God, to manifest good things. Negative, critical words can work just as powerfully as positive, faith-filled words—only in reverse.

IS EVERY CHILD BLESS-ABLE?

Maybe your child is rebellious and you're discouraged. You may be asking, "Am I supposed to bless my child even if he's willfully disobedient and defiant, even if he is a chronic procrastinator, and even if he constantly breaks the rules of our home?"

The answer to this question is an emphatic *yes!* The powerful truth about blessings is this: They don't depend upon the character or condition of the one receiving them. A blessing's true words of value are not linked to a child's performance or outward appearance. Please do not confuse the word *bless* with the word *praise*—because those who need blessing the most are often the ones who deserve praise the least. God acts like this. He sends rain on the righteous and the unrighteous (see Matthew 5:45).

We see an example of this truth in the story of Isaac blessing his sons, Jacob and Esau, in Genesis 27. When Isaac grew old, he knew that he had to give a special blessing to his older son. This was called a birthright. It had nothing to do with the goodness or badness of the son; it was simply his because he was the twin who happened to be born first. But little did Isaac know that Esau, the older son, had foolishly traded his birthright (or the right to the blessing) to his younger brother for a bowl of stew. The incident was forgotten until the day when the aged and nearly blind Isaac called Esau and said he was ready to give the blessing and sent Esau off to hunt an animal and prepare a meal.

Now Isaac's wife, Rebecca, was also in the tent and overheard the conversation. Desiring that her favored son, Jacob, receive the birthright blessing, she quickly devised a plan to trick Isaac. Hurriedly, she and Jacob killed a young goat and prepared a delicious meal. The plan was for Jacob to serve his father the meal and receive the blessing before Esau came back to the tent.

To pull off the scheme, Jacob dressed in his brother's clothing so he would smell like the field and put animal skins on his arms so he would be hairy like Esau. Even though Isaac was a little skeptical because his son's voice sounded like Jacob instead of Esau, he ultimately blessed Jacob with the blessing meant for Esau.

When Esau returned from the field and discovered that he had been robbed of the blessing due him, he let out a loud cry: "Do you have only one blessing, my father? Bless me too!" (Genesis 27:38). Though Isaac did bless Esau also, it was too late to give him the birthright blessing.

Here we see that the person receiving the blessing does not need to be worthy of it. Obviously Jacob lied and was deceptive and greedy, yet, in spite of all this, he received the better blessing.

When we bless our children, we do so not based upon their

achievements but upon God's desires for their lives. This is the reason that we impart blessings "by faith." Hebrews tells us that "by faith" Isaac blessed Jacob and Esau, and "by faith" Jacob blessed each of Joseph's sons (11:20-21).

We bless our children not because of who they are but so they can be all God wants them to be. Blessings bring out the best in others. So start blessing your child and see what God will do!

CONSEQUENCES OF WITHHOLDING BLESSINGS

Why do we withhold blessings? In many homes a thief is loose, robbing us of precious moments to bless our children with words of acceptance. Gary Smalley and John Trent tell us the thief's name is "overactivity" and he masquerades as "fulfillment," "accomplishment," or "success."[6] Just the right time to speak such treasured words is crowded out by a busy schedule.

Earlier in this chapter we noted that God commanded the priests to bless the people. As New Testament believers we are all priests (see 1 Peter 2:9). In this respect, the withholding of blessings goes against part of the essential nature of our purpose as Christians. Withholding blessings from children can:

- cause discouragement, rejection, and offense
- create opportunities for the Enemy to deceive and influence your child through perceived rejection, hurt feelings, condemnation, self-hatred, and bitterness
- dampen his or her desire to please or serve
- block the release of God's favor
- rob joy from you and your children
- create an atmosphere in the home that is spiritually and emotionally cold
- cause you to misrepresent God

- deny them the security and affirmation that they need to grow emotionally strong and healthy
- rob your family of generational blessings

If the truth be known, many parents don't give the blessing because they've never received it themselves. They've never seen it modeled. Perhaps the rule in your family as you were growing up was, "words of love and acceptance are best kept unspoken."

You may be feeling a little inadequate to bless your kids, just as Randy (the dad we mentioned earlier in the chapter) felt at first. You may not feel you have what it takes to do this. Maybe you are guilt-ridden because you don't feel you've been the best parent. Don't let this stop you from freely speaking and praying blessings over your children. Just as a blessing is not dependent upon the condition of the one receiving it, the power of blessing is not dependent upon the one giving it.

In fact, introducing the concept of blessings into your family offers a great opportunity to let your kids know you've not always known what to do, that you've made some mistakes. If this is so, confess it to them, and bless them. They may just come back to you days or years later and tell you how your spoken blessings began to unlock their hearts. Do not abandon your children's hearts by withholding the blessing. Generations to come are counting on you!

THE BLESSING CYCLE

Giving a blessing is like planting seeds. Scripture tells us we reap what we sow (see Galatians 6:7). The more seeds we plant, the more blessings are going to spring up in our own lives and the lives of those around us.

When blessing is modeled in the home, a child is much more likely to end up returning the blessing to his father or mother.

Young people who receive the blessing also start praying for and blessing their siblings, friends, those in their youth group, their teachers, and others. They are more likely to pass on the blessing to their spouses and their children.

This is what Colten Wilson, whose family was mentioned earlier in this chapter, says about the effect of the blessing on his life:

> *My father's blessing is the single most significant tool that is shaping my young life, keeping me focused on my course in what's ahead. How can a young teen grow into a righteous child of God when he is constantly being bombarded by the world about how to look, what to say, how to fit in and be cool? We have got to know our place, who we are, what we are to be. This is the power of the blessing. It is my dad telling me how much he loves me, telling me that I am a man of God—that I am strong, that I am victorious. It is my father speaking over me with his divine authority given to him by God. When I am kneeling in front of my dad, his hands on my head, his eyes looking deep into mine, I can feel his love for me. It is a love that I can never destroy, a love the world can never deprive me of.*
>
> *This love that I get from my father comes from God the Father's love for my dad, which then spills over into my life. Nothing is more life impacting and empowering than that. Bring on the world. I'm under the blessing, protection, and love of my father.*
>
> *As for me, I'll be passing down the blessing to my children, and them to their children, and them to their children. By that time we will have a strong and righteous people under the protection, love, and blessing of their parents—a people that God can use to shake nations for His glory. That is the power of the blessing.*[7]

TAKE IT OUT OF THE HOUSE

We should all look for opportunities to bless children whom God has put in our lives, not just our own children. Many adults who never received the blessing at home say they received these life-changing words and prayers from a coach, teacher, pastor, or youth leader.

For example, I love praying blessings at baby showers. We often ask invitees to bring a written blessing to pray over the expectant mother and her baby still in the womb. Then we place everyone's blessings in a decorative baby book and present it to the mother as a keepsake. Another idea is to record verbal blessings and give a CD to the mother as a gift to pass on to her child in later years.

At an older child's or teenager's birthday party, suggest that everyone gather and pray a blessing over the young person's upcoming year. Even kids who don't know the Lord are usually quite receptive to this.

When your child or another young person in your life is ready to be married, plan a time in the ceremony when you pray blessings over the newlywed couple. My husband and I (Cheryl), along with the groom's parents, gathered around Nicole and Marco and pronounced blessings over them at their wedding.

During a slumber party or campout, invite kids to pray blessings over one another. One Sunday morning we asked the youth group to go over to the children's ministry and pray blessings over the children. Teenagers were just as encouraged by giving blessings as the younger kids were in receiving them.

SATURATE YOUR CHILD IN PRAYER TODAY

*Dear Heavenly Father, please forgive me for the times
I've used my mouth to bring pain rather than blessing to
_____ . Today I bless my child with the assurance of
Your love and mine. I bless _____ with the ability
to hear Your voice and make wise decisions in all the affairs
of life. May he (or she) find favor with both You and others.
I bless my child with the self-discipline to weigh words before
speaking — may everything that comes out of his (or her)
mouth be filled with life, grace, truth, love, and wisdom.
May my child be blessed and a blessing every place he (or
she) goes throughout life. In the name of Jesus Christ I pray.
Amen.*

CHAPTER 4

HEALING PRAYERS FOR HURTING FAMILIES

"But for you who fear my name, the Sun of Righteousness will rise with healing in his wings. And you will go free, leaping with joy like calves let out to pasture." (Malachi 4:2, NLT)

My father loved me and showed me his love in many ways. Nevertheless, I (Cheryl) grew up feeling confused and afraid, because my father also was an alcoholic. Many nights I lay awake in bed listening to my mother and father argue. I was determined that my children would never hear their parents raise their voices or use harsh words with each other.

To my dismay, that was not the case. I was from the South, where the unspoken rules were "Be sweet to everyone. Never, never confront anyone about anything or let anyone outside your home know you have a problem." Hal, who became a Christian as an adult, grew up in an Orthodox Jewish home and was direct and outspoken about everything. Hal and I argued frequently, and in the early years some arguments were quite heated.

One day while Nicole was visiting a friend and I was putting laundry away in her room, I sat down on her bed and began to weep. "Lord," I said, "You know I never wanted Nicole to have to see or hear her parents argue."

The Lord spoke something to my heart at that moment that forever changed the way I parented: He pointed out to me that I couldn't protect Nicole from the problems of life—no family is perfect. However, I could turn mistakes and even painful experiences into opportunities to help her handle in a godly way the problems she would face in life.

Up until this time, when an argument occurred I would interact with Nicole as if nothing had happened. Though Hal and I would reconcile, Nicole rarely saw this side of our relationship. About this time Hal and I discovered a model for asking forgiveness and extending healing prayer. Hal would express to me that he was sorry for his hurtful words and ask my forgiveness. Then he would lay his hand on my heart and pray something like this: "Lord, I've been an instrument of pain to my wife; now I ask You to use me as an instrument of healing. Please heal the wounds that I've inflicted and restore our love and closeness." Then using the same model, I would pray for Hal with words that came from my heart.

As we talked about how powerfully this prayer model impacted our relationship, we both decided that it would be a good idea to include Nicole in these healing prayers. So instead of ignoring the problems, we began to talk to Nicole about them. We let her know we knew our arguing hurt her and made her afraid. We told her we had asked each other for forgiveness. Then we asked her to forgive us, too. The time always ended with one of us putting our hand over her heart and praying that God would heal the wounds we had inflicted and bring our family close together again.

Through the years Hal and I have learned to celebrate each other's differences rather than argue over them. However, had we not prayed with Nicole along life's sometimes difficult journey, she might have grown up wounded and bitter. She might never have learned how to give and receive healing prayer.

Families today suffer a barrage of hurts, conflicts, and challenges. To think or even suggest that daily mealtime or bedtime prayers alone are going to heal deeply entrenched wounds of the heart—in children or in adults—would be simplistic and downright erroneous. But prayer does make a difference. Prayer *does* heal hurting families.

THE KIND OF PRAYER THAT HEALS

There are many different kinds of prayer, including prayers of thanksgiving, intercession, petition, declaration, and spiritual warfare, to name a few. So when we talk about healing prayers for issues of the heart, we mean a specific kind of prayer that accesses the resources of heaven in a way that accomplishes healing.

It's important for us—and our kids—to understand the transactional nature of prayer. When we pray, spiritual activity, which we do not see with our eyes, actually takes place in the heavenly realms. Spiritual activity—with eternal implications—also takes place *within us.*

For example, when we say a prayer to receive Christ as Savior, Scripture tells us we are automatically transferred from the "dominion of darkness" into the "kingdom of [God's] Son" (Colossians 1:13) and are seated with Christ in the heavenly places (see Ephesians 2:6). Old things pass away; we are made new (see 2 Corinthians 5:17). This is a spiritual work we don't see with our physical eyes, although we experience the fruit of it: being filled with the Spirit, hearing God's voice, and experiencing power in our prayers and peace in our hearts.

At the same time, we continue to live in a fallen world and are subject to diverse assaults of the Enemy (see 1 Peter 5:8). We encounter disappointment, rejection, and fear. We experience broken relationships, broken bodies, and broken homes. We suffer lost jobs, lost children, and lost dreams. Christian families are certainly not exempt from these struggles.

Healing prayer is a provision God has made for us to overcome the continual assaults of sin, the world we live in, and our enemy, the Devil. Jesus came to set us free (see Luke 4:18-19)! And we can appropriate that healing and freedom — for ourselves and our children — through *prayer*. Healing prayers go to the wounds in our hearts and release God's mercy and love, similar to the way salvation prayer goes to the brokenness in our spirits and releases God's grace and forgiveness.

ROOTS AND FRUITS

Many times, when we pray with and for our families about hurtful situations, what we should be praying about are the root causes of those problems. When best-selling author Stormie O'Martian became a mom, she was worried that some of the negative patterns of her difficult childhood would show up in her own parenting. She battled the "fruit" of the problem first — trying to control feelings and behaviors. But it wasn't until she went to the root of the problem that she was able to break free. She relates:

> *I sensed feelings of rage and rejection rising up in me. I realized I was a potential child abuser. It was built in from childhood because of my mother's violent abuse of me. The only way I could cope with this frightening revelation was to spend a lot of time in the Lord's presence. Each time I fell before Him in utter guilt and failure, His love came upon me like a healing balm. Each time I cried out to Him for deliverance, He faithfully set me free. Eventually I was completely freed from my anger and*

feelings of rejection, and I learned how powerful, how merci-
ful, how tender, and how complete His presence is. I finally
came to understand the depth of God's love toward me.[1]

When we let overt sin, sinful responses, or even negative
emotions remain with us, whether they be rejection and rage—as
Stormie experienced—or anger, hurt, fear, disappointment, or any
other feelings the circumstances provoke, we give the Devil a foothold (see Ephesians 4:26-27). Left unchecked, footholds evolve
into strongholds—deeply ingrained habits, wrong thoughts, and
belief systems that "[set themselves] up against the knowledge of
God" (2 Corinthians 10:4-5), and exert a dominating influence in
our lives and homes. How can this not affect our children?

The fruits of these strongholds show up in what we might call
overt issues such as sexual immorality, stealing, lying, addictions,
drunkenness, angry outbursts, violence, abuse, and so on. Yet the
roots of strongholds are generally built up subtly through sins of
the heart such as bitterness, unforgiveness, anger, and shame.
Many times, these fruits (or behaviors) started out as coping
mechanisms by which we protected ourselves from abuse, rejection, disappointment, and fear. But as we continued in them as
a way of life, they grew to function as wide-open doors for the
Enemy in our lives, and our children bear the effects.

GROWN-UPS GO FIRST

When the flight attendant gives the safety speech at the beginning of every plane flight, we hear something like, "In the event of
a loss of cabin pressure, oxygen masks will drop from the ceiling.
Please secure your own mask first before assisting your children."
We can directly apply this principle to healing prayer. We can best
accomplish or effect healing in our families when we are willing

to start with ourselves first.

It's not possible to list all the situations in which families might encounter serious pain from which they need healing, but here are a few:

- Addictions (alcohol, drugs, pornography, gambling, etc.)
- Adoption, foster care situations
- Death
- Divorce, blended families
- Effects of emotional, physical, or sexual abuse
- Fighting
- Injustice
- Loss of job or income
- Prodigals
- Serious illnesses, disabilities, or accidents
- Extramarital pregnancies and/or abortion

In all these things, what arises in the hearts of adults and children alike are things mentioned earlier, like rejection, unforgiveness, bitterness, and fear. Prayerfully ask the Holy Spirit to reveal to you ways that these root issues may be in your own heart. Ask others to pray with and for you. Be humble and teachable rather than defensive.

On this level, prayer for real healing can take place.

FREEDOM IN FORGIVENESS

Jesus warned that opportunities for offenses, stumbling blocks, and temptations are inevitable (see Matthew 18:7). But it's not inevitable that we let them settle in our hearts and homes. When we give a place to bitterness, we inadvertently teach our children that it's okay to live with unforgiveness. On the other hand, when we set the example of keeping short accounts — of constantly and consistently going to the root of heart issues and forgiving and releasing our offenders — we help children establish lifelong patterns of emotional health and wholeness.

Extending forgiveness doesn't necessarily mean that relationships become immediately rosy again. Forgiveness means that you release someone from a debt you feel he or she owes you and, in the process, you are released, as well.

Arlyn's friend Karan lived for years with deep anger and bitterness toward her ex-husband. Christmastime was particularly difficult, when she had to surrender her three boys to him and his new wife for the holidays. One Christmas Eve, as she was begrudgingly preparing her children for their holiday visit, she cried out to the Lord to deliver her from her bitterness.

"Give him the china," she sensed the Holy Spirit say.

When he left, her husband had taken half of their china to his new home. Now Karan sensed God telling her to wrap up her half, write "Merry Christmas" on the box, and send it along with the children as a gift.

As she placed the package in her children's arms, the burden of bitterness, anger, and resentment was suddenly and miraculously lifted from her heart. Her bitterness was replaced by heartfelt compassion and a desire to pray for her ex-husband with her children and to bless him. In her freedom, she was able to help her children resolve their own bitterness and be free to develop loving relationships with both of their parents.

TEACHING CHILDREN TO RESOLVE BITTERNESS

Prayer can help train children to deal with the root issues behind sibling conflicts, to learn self-control, and to extend forgiveness to one another. Prayer helped my husband, Hal, and me discern the root issue behind a physical malady Nicole suffered when she was in elementary school, one that otherwise might have led to a drastic medical intervention. Nicole complained of burning in her stomach, nausea, and being unable to eat. She had every symptom of a stomach ulcer. So we took her to a gastroenterologist. Though tests revealed no ulcer, sure enough, an irritation in the lining of the stomach showed up. Several hundred dollars in doctor bills later, no cause or solution for the problem had been discovered.

During this time, Nicole missed a great deal of school and was falling behind in her work. Hal and I were praying together daily, asking God to heal Nicole's stomach, yet the problem persisted. One night as Nicole lay on the sofa, wrapped in a blanket and complaining about how sick she felt, Hal moved to her side so he could talk and pray with her. Within a few moments, it was as if lights came on in Hal's spirit.

"Nicole, could it be that you are harboring resentment toward someone, and that's the reason God is not answering our prayers?"

Nicole broke into tears. Immediately Nicole thought of Jamie, a new girl who had recently enrolled in Nicole's school. Jamie had begun, at first, to "hang out" with Nicole and her best friend. However, within a short while, tension began to develop between Nicole and the new girl. It seemed they each felt threatened by the other. Nicole repented right then and there. Within hours, the stomach pain diminished and Nicole steadily grew better each day.

NATURAL PROBLEMS, SPIRITUAL ROOTS

It's true: Sometimes issues of the heart and spirit affect our physical bodies. Arlyn experienced this phenomenon when she and Doug took their family on a road trip from their home in Washington

State to California, where the main attraction was Disneyland. Within hours after arriving, Doug became physically ill to the point of not being able to get out of bed. Arlyn recalls,

In the morning Doug was no better, and I dreaded the prospect of lugging five active children around a crowded theme park all by myself. We all gathered around the bed, laid our hands on Doug, and each offered a prayer that God would heal him. Interestingly enough (and I can't remember now who prayed it), one of us prayed in the name of Jesus that any schemes of the Enemy against Doug or our family would be exposed and defeated. Then we all trooped dejectedly downstairs to catch the shuttle to Disneyland, leaving behind a very miserable daddy.

At the bus stop where our hotel's shuttle would pick us up, Tyler (then sixteen) had a stricken look on his face.

"Mom," he said urgently, "stay here. Don't get on the shuttle. I'll be right back." Then he dashed back toward our room—and didn't return for twenty minutes. When he did come back, he had his dad in tow!

The Holy Spirit had spoken to Tyler after we prayed for Doug, pointing out to him some attitudes and heart issues in Doug that had evidenced themselves on our trip over the past few days. Tyler had the clear sense that these had been a "foothold" for the Enemy (see Ephesians 4:26-27) to try to ruin our family's time together.

In tears (because he was feeling understandably awkward bringing this message to his dad), Tyler told Doug what he was hearing from the Lord. Doug had the humility to recognize and admit that Ty was right. He confessed the sin, repented, received God's forgiveness, and asked the Holy Spirit to fill him and help him walk in the opposite spirit. Doug came down to the shuttle to join the rest of the family, and by the time we got to Disneyland, he felt fine. We stayed

until the park closed, watched the fireworks, and had a mar-
velous time!

When we pray about whether a physical problem has a spiritual
root, we rely on the Holy Spirit to point it out in *His* timing and try
to be sensitive to what He may be saying. We should never impose
the idea of a spiritual root on someone else, but always humbly
submit it to the person for prayerful consideration. Even as a parent
to a child, we can say what we hear the Lord saying, but it is still
the child's responsibility to repent if repentance is due. More often
than not, our primary responsibility when we discern a root issue is
to *intercede*—that it will be exposed and that the person concerned
(parent or child) will hear God's voice and respond.

PRAYING ABOUT SERIOUS ILLNESSES

When an illness is not the *result* of spiritual issues, it can certainly
be the *cause* of them. In the face of serious illness, God wants to
heal families of things like fear, anger, hopelessness, or sorrow,
which may be associated with an illness.

Fear was certainly an issue when Michael's dad, Jeff, gave
Michael a bedtime hug and felt a lump on Michael's arm bone near
his shoulder. Cheri Fuller tells the story in her book *When Families
Pray.* For Michael and his parents, a lump caused great concern.
You see, although only seven, Michael was a cancer survivor.

When he was less than a year old, Michael had endured
aggressive chemotherapy, radiation, and a bone marrow transplant
to treat a rapidly advancing case of leukemia. His family faced the
uncertainty of Michael's health and the burden of a $205,000 bill
for the bone marrow transplant, a procedure their insurance didn't
cover. But they had seen God's faithfulness over and over. Not
only did Michael's cancer go into remission, but God also pro-

vided for his care through a community that rallied to raise the money for the transplant.

Now an X-ray showed a mass on the bone, and in a few days Michael would undergo further tests at a children's hospital in Portland, Oregon.

When Michael had leukemia he was too young to know what was happening. This time, he was old enough to be a little worried. Kristi found herself turning to 1 Peter 5:6-7. "Humble yourselves, therefore, under God's mighty hand, that he may lift you up in due time. Cast all your anxiety on him because he cares for you," she read. Kristi explained to Michael, "Whatever bothers you, any problem or worry, Jesus wants to take it because He loves you even more than Mommy and Daddy do, and we love you so much!"

Then Kristi asked her son a familiar question: "What does this verse mean to *you*, honey?"

"It means I can put Mr. Lump in Jesus' hands, and I don't have to worry!" Michael replied, his blue eyes sparkling with confidence.

His mom's heart leaped. This seven-year-old understood for himself Peter's exhortation. Most importantly, he trusted God. After that day, Michael truly didn't worry. Michael possessed an amazing, simple trust that enabled him to leave his lump with Jesus, whereas most of us are tempted to pick up our "lumps," take them back, carry them ourselves, or try to help God fix them.

A week later, Michael underwent a series of tests: a CAT scan, a bone scan, an ultrasound, and later an MRI. From that evidence, the doctors told the family they believed the lump was a benign mass produced from previous chemotherapy and radiation and nothing to worry about. But Michael already knew not to worry. He'd given his lump to Jesus.[2]

CONQUERING FEAR THROUGH PRAYER

Because children are small and the world is big, strong emotions —such as fear—can be giants in a child's life. It's important to help children identify their fears and learn to replace them with faith in God's provision and protection. Children fear things ranging from thunder and lightning to imaginary monsters under their beds to new situations like starting school or riding the bus for the first time. Or, like Michael, there may be issues about which they have genuine reason to be concerned. When we call their fears "foolish," we only reinforce their insecurity. But when we take their concerns seriously and help them take their anxiety to their heavenly Father, we let them know that they matter to us and to God, and that they are never really alone.

Ask the Lord to show you if your child's fear, anger, or sorrow is an emotional reaction or if it is spiritually rooted. If it is spiritually rooted, ask Him to show you where. Then intercede that the root be exposed and the child be willing to recognize and turn away from it.

PRAYING FOR PRODIGALS

A friend of Arlyn's struggled to understand how and why his grown son ended up the way he did. As a young child, the son evidenced a heart for God. As an adult—unkempt, tattooed, and rebellious—the young man was a constant source of concern, even embarrassment, to his parents. After yet another prayer during which the father relayed his frustration to God over the seeming lack of progress in his son's life, the Holy Spirit spoke.

"You're missing what I'm doing in your son's life," the father sensed God saying. "You're so focused on what you see with your physical eyes that you don't see what I see."

Immediately the father repented. He began to thank God for who He had created his son to be and for what He was doing in his life—even if he and his wife couldn't see it.

Shortly thereafter, the son contacted his parents, asking, "You've changed the way you've been praying for me, haven't you?" The parents told him yes. "Well, keep it up," said the young man. His parents couldn't have been more surprised!

Praying for a prodigal who has wandered away from God or for a child who wants nothing to do with your faith can be a frustrating and painful experience. In these cases, healing prayers are needed not just for the children themselves, but also on behalf of the parents, friends, and family members who are praying for them.

Here are some healing prayers for these kinds of hurting families:

- **Thankfulness**—Yes, thankfulness! Be thankful for everything God is doing, whether you can see it or not. He is in control.
- **Forgiveness**—Forgive your child for the fear he or she has caused you, for the loss of your dreams, reputation, or family harmony. Forgive yourself for any regrets you have about your parenting, choices you made, or things you wish you'd done differently.
- **God's Word**—Find specific passages that speak of God's promises for you, your child, your spouse, and your other children. Rephrase them into prayers that take the focus off the painful situation and put it on the Lord.
- **God's Perspective**—Ask God to show you what He is doing in your child's life. Acknowledge that He is God, that He created your child with a design and destiny, and that He is the one who will complete the good work He began in that child's life (see Philippians 1:6).
- **Spiritual Warfare**—Declare Christ's authority and victory

over the Enemy's schemes against your children (see Isaiah 54:17; Luke 10:19; 2 Corinthians 2:11). Pray that the veil the Enemy has used to blind them to the truth of God's love and salvation be removed (see 2 Corinthians 4:4), along with any obstacles that prevent them from humbling themselves to receive forgiveness and restoration.

- **Softening of the heart**—Ask that the Holy Spirit draw the child to the Father's heart. Pray that he or she will run *to* God and not *away* from Him.
- **Self-surrender**—Take your eyes off the child as the problem and ask God, "Lord, what do You want to do in *me*?" Let yourself be refined and transformed.

The story of Joseph in Genesis 37–50 is a tremendous encouragement to hurting families. Despite poor parenting, extreme sibling rivalry, bitter conflict, and shocking betrayal, God's purposes prevailed and the family was healed and restored. "What you meant for evil," Joseph told his brothers, "God used for good" (see Genesis 50:20). This is the prayer, the hope, and the promise for all hurting families. Whatever the Enemy has meant for evil, God can (and will) surely use for good.

TAKE IT OUT OF THE HOUSE

Does your church have a prayer support group for families of prodigals? If not, consider starting one. These families need special spiritual and emotional care—and sometimes even practical support when a child acts out, lands in jail, or becomes pregnant. Sometimes deep feelings of shame and embarrassment will cause them to isolate themselves or to put on a happy face that serves to mask the pain they're really feeling. Be sensitive to people in your congregation who may be experiencing these kinds of situations. Pray for their marriages and their relationships with other children. Be someone they can be honest with about how things are really going without fear of your judgment. Your prayers and encouragement will serve to bear their burden—which fulfills the law of Christ (see Galatians 6:2).

SATURATE YOUR CHILD WITH PRAYER TODAY

Dear Heavenly Father, please heal my family from the hurts we've experienced and even inflicted on one another. Help us release all bitterness, strife, anger, unforgiveness, fear, and competition. Put Your finger on root issues in our hearts that cause us to bring hurt and shame to ourselves and one another. Help each one of us invite You into the most painful places of our lives—those places we haven't wanted to look at. Soften and heal our hearts. Give me insight into how to pray, and wisdom to deal with relational issues in my family in a way that pleases You. Amen.

CHAPTER 5

CLOSING DOORS TO THE ENEMY

Stay alert! Watch out for your great enemy, the devil. He prowls around like a roaring lion, looking for someone to devour. Stand firm against him, and be strong in your faith. (1 Peter 5:8-9, NLT)

"Mommyyyy!"

Hillary's tiny voice screeched through the house, rousing me (Arlyn) from yet another good night's sleep. For the past month, three-year-old Hillary and her six-year-old brother, Timothy, had been waking up nearly every night, gripped with fear. A few times we had even found Hillary wandering around the house in the dead of night, crying—fast asleep!

"Lord," I prayed, "our kids are usually peaceful sleepers. They don't read scary books or watch horror movies. What's going on?"

Doug and I had only recently become aware of the reality of spiritual warfare and the power of the Holy Spirit that was available to us through our authority in Jesus Christ. Hillary and Timothy's night terrors directly coincided with a concerted effort on our part to introduce these principles into the fabric of our family's prayer life. This was our first real opportunity to apply in our own family what we'd been learning at church.

When we told our pastor about the children's night terrors, he suggested we "pray through" our house—do a little "spiritual housecleaning," of sorts. This seemed like a good idea. Besides, nothing else had worked! So Doug and I spent some time praying together, asking the Lord to show us if there was anything in our home that might be granting access—an open door—to the Enemy to torment our children.

As we prayed, two things came to mind. One was a nearly life-sized cutout of a menacing character from a science fiction movie that Doug had brought home from work and placed in the children's play room. The other thing that came to mind was less obvious. While we were praying, Doug kept seeing a picture in his mind of a strange, animated creature. When he described it, none of the children had any idea what it was or what it might represent.

Doug asked Tyler, our oldest son, if he still had any trading cards lying around. (We had already done a clean sweep of these, some of which we felt portrayed images of demonic creatures.) Tyler said he'd gotten rid of them all. Still, Doug continued to feel drawn toward Tyler's room. One day, he decided to pull everything out of the closet and give it a thorough search. There he found a card box stuffed with sports cards. Buried in the midst of the sports cards was one lone card with an image very similar to the one Doug had seen!

"Lord," we prayed together, "we're sorry we've let the kids play with things that are unholy because we didn't really believe the Enemy had power through them. And we ask Your forgiveness for fearing the children's reaction more than we feared Yours."

We then went through each room in the house, asking the Lord to show us what might be offensive to Him. We got rid of anything that the Holy Spirit highlighted to us and anointed the rooms with oil as a symbol of consecration to the Lord and as an invitation to the Holy Spirit's presence.

We also began praying over our children when they went to bed at night—not just praying *with* them, but praying *over* them. We asked that God's angels surround and protect them. We bound the Enemy, in Jesus' name, from tormenting them with nightmares or terrors. The children eventually picked up on this and began praying that way themselves each night: "No bad thoughts and dreams—in Jesus' name, amen!"

The night terrors stopped completely and have never returned.

OPEN DOORS THROUGH DEFILING OBJECTS AND ACTIVITIES

Does the idea of needing to close open doors to the Enemy—"spiritual housecleaning"—sound far-fetched to you? It shouldn't. When we pray for our kids, we have to resist our human tendency to look at people and situations only through physical eyes and instead look at them with spiritual eyes. We must be alert to what may be going on in the heavenly realms, as well as in the natural realm. This may be partly what Paul had in mind when he said, "For our struggle is not against flesh and blood, but against the rulers, against the authorities, against the powers of this dark world and against the spiritual forces of evil in the heavenly realms" (Ephesians 6:12).

Scripture gives many examples of situations in which doors were opened to the Enemy in a family or community through defiling objects and activities. In Genesis 31, Jacob, not knowing that his wife, Rachel, had stolen her father's household idols, boldly asserted, "If you find anyone who has your gods, *he shall not live*" (verse 32, emphasis added). Rachel deceptively kept the idols hidden so her father would not find them during a search (see Genesis 31:35). She may have felt that it was not a big deal or that she had gotten away with something. But years later she did, indeed, die a premature death (see Genesis 35:16-19).

In Joshua 6:17-19, God commanded the Israelites not to take any spoil when they laid siege to the city of Jericho. Later, when the Israelite army went up against the village of Ai in battle (which should have been an easy conquest), they were soundly defeated. On inquiring of the Lord why this had happened, they learned that their camp had been defiled when Achan brought stolen property into their camp. It was not until after the objects in question had been exposed and removed that the curse was lifted and Israel was once more victorious in battle.

This principle was enacted in a positive light in the New Testament when the Ephesian Christians "who had practiced sorcery brought their scrolls together and burned them publicly" (Acts 19:19). The passage goes on to highlight the result of the cleansing: "In this way the word of the Lord spread widely and grew in power" (verse 20). We can surely expect the same results when we model the same faith and obedience!

Scripture warns us to "be on the alert" because our enemy, Satan, is like a "roaring lion looking for someone to devour" (1 Peter 5:8). Many of us have been lulled into a false sense of security about this. Like the proverbial ostrich, we Western Christians tend to have our heads in the sand about how much influence the Enemy really can have over our lives. Because of our largely naturalistic mind-set, we tend to dismiss the idea that mere objects can have any influence on us, our homes, or our children. But they can — and sometimes they do.

It's not just idols and voodoo feathers that we need to worry about. Occultic or sexually themed movies, certain books and magazines, violent and demonic video and computer games or cartoons — all these can be the very doors through which the Enemy gains access to influence our children. His goal is to obstruct, oppose, corrupt, pervert, and harass the work and people of God.

What kinds of objects might open the door of your home to

the Enemy? These might include the following:

- **Images** of spirits, idols, foreign gods, and demonic creatures, which can include pictures, posters, and statues
- **Symbols,** books, jewelry, and implements of false religions or secret societies
- **Occult objects**—anything related to the occult, including Ouija boards, horoscopes, fortune-telling paraphernalia, witchcraft, voodoo, New Age, etc.
- **Items with themes** that are inappropriately sexual, violent, rebellious, or demonic, including books, movies, music, video games, and magazines
- **Personal links** to past sins, immoral relationships, or violations (emotional, physical, or sexual), such as photos, correspondence, jewelry, gifts, and diaries or journals
- **Excessive identification with worldly culture**—This is an area of personal freedom and discernment, but watch for affiliation with worldly or destructive mind-sets such as materialism, Goth or "punk" mentality and dress, heavy metal music and/or lifestyle, drug culture, and so on.

OPEN DOORS THROUGH DEFILING ACTIVITIES

Elaine awakened to the screams of her son and wearily shuffled down the hall to Joey's room. This was becoming all too familiar. In Joey's room, she comforted her sweat-soaked son. As she had so many other nights, she soothed him and assured him of her presence.

Elaine had reached her limit. When daylight came, Elaine called her friend Joan, who suggested praying through Joey's room. As they did so later that day, Joan sensed something in the room was truly wrong. A picture formed in her mind of a child being beaten in that room.

Elaine was stunned. Joey's night terrors were often triggered by dreams of someone beating him. Joan grabbed Elaine's hand and knelt by the bed to ask God to forgive the sin of child abuse that had happened in that room. With authority in her voice, Joan commanded the evil presence to leave. The room brightened, and Elaine felt a peace she hadn't felt in that room.

A few weeks later, Elaine was talking with a neighbor who had known the previous occupants of the house. She related that she sometimes heard yelling and that the police had come several times. She believed that eventually the child had been removed from the home.[1]

Spiritual doors to the Enemy can be opened through sinful, hurtful activities in a physical or geographic location, such as a home. These doors can be identified and slammed shut through prayer. Sometimes the Holy Spirit will reveal open doors through an impression, which may feel like a "gut feeling" or instinct. It may come in mental pictures as you are praying. Other times you will be aware through natural knowledge of potential open doors to the Enemy's influence in a home or other building.

CLOSING DOORS OPENED BY DEFILING OBJECTS AND ACTIVITIES

If you're going to do some spiritual housecleaning—slam the door in the Enemy's face and pull in the welcome mat, so to speak—here are some steps you and your family can take:

1. **Assess your home through spiritual eyes.** Room by room, prayerfully go through your house and take note of anything that the Holy Spirit would not want there. Ask Him to reveal to you, either by a prompting in your spirit

or through natural knowledge, any defiling activities or sin that have occurred there.

2. **Remove or destroy** anything that you sense might grant an open door to the Enemy. Renounce any involvement you or your family have had with that object or any activity associated with it. Ask for — and receive — God's forgiveness.

3. **Command any spiritual forces** that have been granted access to your home through defiling objects or activities to be gone, in the name of Jesus (see Matthew 4:10; Luke 10:19; James 4:7).

4. **Pray for the cleansing power and presence of the Holy Spirit** to permeate that room and your whole house. You may want to use oil to anoint the doors, windows, or furniture (anointing oil is available in most Christian bookstores and catalogs). Oil can be a reminder of the cleansing blood of Jesus, as well as a symbol of the Holy Spirit Himself.

5. **Refill your rooms** and household with objects and activities of God's presence, glory, and holiness. Play worship music. Pray together as a family in different rooms of the house. Make declarations, in the name and authority of Jesus, that your house belongs to the Lord. Proclaim aloud, as Joshua did: "As for me and my household, we will serve the Lord!" (Joshua 24:15).

OPEN DOORS THROUGH GENERATIONAL SIN

Family resemblances are funny things. Sometimes they're genetic, like my (Arlyn's) son's curly hair or the peculiar extra vertebra I have at the base of my spine (that gene courtesy of my Scottish maternal ancestors). Sometimes they're learned traits, like my husband's idiosyncratic way of wrinkling his nose under his glasses, the way his dad always does. I came away from my own family of origin with my father's cleft chin, my sister's laugh, and my mother's funny toes.

Regrettably, family resemblances can sometimes be negative. People can be genetically predisposed to physical and emotional defects and disorders: asthma, cancer, and diabetes; anxiety, depression, and mental illness. Destructive patterns such as anger, neglect, poverty, adultery, illegitimacy, addiction, and abuse often proliferate throughout families—even Christian families—from generation to generation.

Many families find themselves faced with issues that, despite all efforts to the contrary, seem to stubbornly resist change and healing. We counsel, we intervene, we pray, we intercede; we try every way we know to change the cycle—yet the patterns continue, stubbornly defying physical, psychological, or spiritual intervention. Doors seem to remain open to the Enemy, despite efforts to close them. Why might that be?

One Christian family helplessly watched their teenage son progress from using nicotine to marijuana to heroin—then become addicted. They prayed. Their extended family and church family prayed. Occasionally, the boy would repent and try to get clean, but each time he would fall back into drugs and into stealing to support his habit.

One day in prayer the Holy Spirit brought to the mind of the boy's uncle that previous generations of his family had been marked by alcoholism and bootlegging. When he questioned older family members, this proved to be true. Although their own branch of the family had been Christians and alcohol-free for two generations, previous generations had been ravaged by addiction. Upon closer observation of the extended family, there were indications that the problem was still present—it had simply been "Christianized" into more acceptable compulsive behaviors and addictions. In fact, the uncle had been freed from an addiction himself a few years earlier.

Were all these things related? Was there a correlation between the patterns of previous generations and those of today? Was it possible that the sins of the past had cast a shadow of addiction on this family?

GENERATIONAL SHADOWS

Some problems may seem to stubbornly resist healing and change, because they are spiritually energized by the Enemy through open doors that are generational in nature—like the addiction in our friend's extended family. Just as a shadow cast by one person can cause darkness to fall on another person, the sins of the generations that preceded us can have spiritual repercussion in our families' lives today.

The concept of generational sin is often difficult for contemporary Western Christians to swallow, perhaps because we live in such an individualistic society. Unlike other cultures that are more community oriented, we Westerners find it harder to accept that we bear responsibility for the behavior of others. We tend to deny that our actions can have deep spiritual impact on the people around us. However, there is evidence, both Scriptural and practical, that the spiritual impact of sin can be shared by a family or community and even passed on from generation to generation.

For example, in Joshua 7, when Achan took forbidden plunder from the city of Jericho, God's hand of judgment went against the entire Israelite community. Similarly, when David sought the Lord regarding a famine that had been plaguing the land for three years, God told him it was the result of generational sin (see 2 Samuel 21:1-9).

Subsequent generations may indeed live in the shadows of sin committed by their parents, grandparents, or great-grandparents. For example, you may know of an alcoholic grandfather whose son and grandson also became alcoholics, or a grandmother who became an unwed mother at a young age and whose daughter and granddaughter followed her down the same path, even though they vowed they wouldn't. While Scripture is clear that each person is individually responsible for the guilt of his or her own sin, it also reveals that families and communities bear the spiritual consequences of sins committed in their midst.

When our friend's nephew finally consented to intervention for his heroin addiction, the uncle simultaneously intervened on a spiritual level. Over the course of several days, he went before the Lord in prayer: fasting, repenting, and interceding. As Daniel and Nehemiah did, he intervened before the Lord, identifying himself with the sins of addiction that had been characteristic of himself, his extended family, and previous generations. In warfare prayer, he closed the doors to the Enemy, portals that had allowed this pattern to be energized from generation to generation. And something powerful happened.

The boy's doctors were amazed. His withdrawal from heroin was surprisingly painless, one of the easiest they'd seen. Years later, he is still clean.

When families, in faith, take the responsibility of repentance upon themselves for doors opened to the Enemy in previous generations, God honors and blesses those prayers, just as it says in Leviticus: "But if they will confess their sins and the sins of their fathers—their treachery against me and their hostility toward me . . . I will remember my covenant with Jacob and my covenant with Isaac and my covenant with Abraham, and I will remember the land" (Leviticus 26:40-42).

How can we know if a sin is generational and can thus affect our children's future? There are several possible indicators:

- *Experience*—The problem stubbornly resists genuine attempts on the individual's part to change, including prayer, counseling, or medical intervention.

- *Observation and research* — The problem can be seen in other family members in various forms and degrees. Older family members confirm it has been an issue in past generations. Look at your family tree. Try to identify addictions or besetting sins that are (or were) characteristic in the lives of family members. Can you see any patterns?

- *Discernment* — You have a Holy Spirit sensitivity that "there's more to this than meets the eye." Jesus seemed to rely on such discernment to ascertain that the blind man's infirmity was *not generational* (see John 9:3).

- *Prophetic revelation* — The Holy Spirit speaks clearly and definitely in prayer or grants a word of knowledge (see 1 Corinthians 12:8), either to you or to another person, that the sin issue is generational in nature. He may or may not reveal the original source. Sometimes the original access point of the sin into the family line is so far back that there is no memory of it in current generations. In this case, revelation has to be acted upon in faith.

CLOSING GENERATIONAL DOORS

Here is a model for how you might pray through sin issues, whether generational or otherwise. This is not a form to replace your own Spirit-led conversation with the Lord. It is simply a tool to help you. If your children are old enough to understand, they can pray with you as well.[2]

1. Repent of the sin. Call it what it is. It may be a heart attitude, like bitterness, rebellion, or pride. It could be a behavior, like alcohol abuse, immorality, or stealing. In instances in which you have been wounded or abused, the sin is not the offense committed against you. The sin is your (or your child's) own human response to it — unforgiveness or bitterness, for example. Recognize these as sin responses and confess them. Then grant forgiveness from your heart to the offender.

Sample Prayer: Lord, I repent of the sin of _____.
I accept responsibility on behalf of our generations by confessing and repenting of this sin. I identify myself with it and ask for your forgiveness. I forgive those who have wronged me and entrust them to You to deal with, and release them from any obligation or debt toward me.

"Repent, then, and turn to God, so that your sins may be wiped out, that times of refreshing may come from the Lord" (Acts 3:19).

2. Rebuke the Enemy. Rebuke any influence of the Enemy in your life (and your family's lives) because of this sin, through the power of Jesus' death and resurrection and in the authority of His name. Jesus did this in Matthew 4:10 when He said, "Away from me, Satan!" Paul rebuked evil in Acts 16:18 when he commanded an evil spirit to stop tormenting a young girl. As Jesus' disciples, we have this authority, too, both in our lives and the lives of our children (see Luke 10:19).

Sample Prayer: Like Jesus, I command any influence of the Enemy through the sin of _____
to be gone, in Jesus' name and authority. In Jesus' name, I close the door to the Enemy that has been open in our family because of this sin and I dispel the shadows it has cast over the generations.

"Submit yourselves, then, to God. Resist the devil, and he will flee from you" (James 4:7).

3. Replace the old. Attitudes, actions, and emotions that have been energized by the Enemy need to be replaced with ones that reflect the heart and character of Jesus Christ and the truth of God's Word. Prayerfully and obediently develop a new lifestyle.

Sample Prayer: Lord, I replace the old way of thinking and acting with thoughts and actions that are consistent with Your Word and Your character. Name these specifically. For example, replace fear and/or control with faith and trust. Replace pride with humility. Replace anger with compassion and so on. Help your child replace selfishness with generosity.

"You were taught, with regard to your former way of life, to put off your old self, which is being corrupted by its deceitful desires; to be made new in the attitude of your minds; and to put on the new self, created to be like God in true righteousness and holiness" (Ephesians 4:22-24).

4. Receive God's forgiveness and cleansing. Alone or with your child, ask God to fill you anew with His Holy Spirit to strengthen you to think, behave, and feel rightly.

Sample Prayer: Lord, I receive Your forgiveness. Thank You for Your mercy and compassion toward me. Thank You that You remove my sin as far as the east is from the west. Please fill me with Your Holy Spirit and give me the strength and power to live in the truth, in obedience, and in freedom from now on.

Paul said, "Be filled with the Spirit" (Ephesians 5:18).

TAKE IT OUT OF THE HOUSE

When our church moved into a new building that was many years old, prayer teams spent many days and evenings praying through the building and closing spiritual doors through which the Enemy might attempt to bring opposition to the work of God there.

In one particular section of the building, the prayer teams sensed dark oppression and had impressions of child abuse and great fear. In faith they interceded against these, commanded any presence of the Enemy to be gone in Jesus' name, and prayed for the peaceful presence of the Holy Spirit to permeate those rooms. They prayed that the rooms would be a haven of God's comfort, joy, and love to the children who would come there to learn to know Jesus. They later discovered through longtime residents of the area and old newspaper accounts that there had, indeed, been a terrible child abuse scandal there many years earlier. When people who knew those rooms previously visit them now, they report that there is a perceptible difference in the spiritual environment or the "feel" of the rooms. The darkness and heaviness are completely gone, and there is a genuine sense of fun, joy, and the peaceful presence of the Lord there.

SATURATE YOUR CHILD WITH PRAYER TODAY

Lord God, I thank You for Your promise that You have given us authority over all the power of the Enemy and that no weapon of his that is launched against us will stand (see Luke 10:19; Isaiah 54:17). I do declare that my household and I will serve You and You alone, and that we and our children are under the protection of the precious blood of Jesus. I ask You to show me any open door in my life, my home, or my generation that would give the Enemy an opportunity to oppose, torment, or afflict me and my children. In the power and authority of Jesus, I shut those doors to the Enemy. Oh Lord, I ask for the peaceful presence of Your Spirit to rule in my home and the protection of Your angels to encircle my home — and my children — at all times. In Jesus' name I pray, amen.

CHAPTER 6

PRAYER TRAINING 101

We will not hide these truths from our children;
>   we will tell the next generation
about the glorious deeds of the Lord,
>   about his power and his mighty wonders, . . .
so the next generation might know them —
>   even the children not yet born —
>   and they in turn will teach their own children.
(Psalm 78:4,6, NLT)

During the years Nicole was a preschooler my life was extremely busy. With our growing ministry headquartered in our home, I (Cheryl) felt my personal and family life was being encroached upon. Our fax machine and copier were stationed in our master bedroom and the kitchen table served as my desk. My time was consumed by serving as a personal assistant to my husband along with my own teaching ministry, keeping up our home, and running after a three-year-old.

It seemed the only time I had to spend alone with the Lord was very early in the morning. I would often awake at 4:00 a.m., slip out of bed, and tiptoe down the hall past Nicole's room to the living room couch to pray while peering out the picture window into the quiet night sky. No matter how carefully I crept past Nicole's door, it was usually only a matter of minutes until I heard the pitter-patter of little feet and saw her silhouette appear in the doorway with pillow and blanket dragging behind.

"What are you doing, Mommy?" she would ask.

"I'm praying, honey! This is Mommy's time to talk to God."

At first I tried to coerce her into going back to bed. At this stage in my life I didn't recognize I was about to miss a wonderful opportunity to invite Nicole into my "prayer closet"—to demonstrate my love for God and model a life of prayer. After I began to realize that all of my prayer time would be used up in a battle of getting her back to bed, I began inviting Nicole to sit quietly with me during my prayer time. Wrapped in a warm blanket, she would snuggle next to me and listen as I whispered my prayers to God. Sometimes she would fall asleep beside me. More often than not, the first glimmer of morning sun would find us sitting together in the presence of the Lord.

Hal, on the other hand, would usually go for a prayerwalk in the evenings. Nicole still talks about how she enjoyed riding on her daddy's shoulders as he walked our neighborhood and poured out his heart to God.

I've heard it said many times that prayer is more "caught" than "taught." If this is true, then welcoming children into our prayer times is one of the best ways to ensure that we pass on a legacy of prayer to the next generation.

Keith Wooden, in his book *Teaching Children to Pray*, says, "A 'prayer closet' that is open to the intrusive chatter of children may be the best opportunity you have to demonstrate your reverence and love for God. Invite them into your Holy of Holies to savor the presence of the Lord with you." Children need to have a sense that God lives in their home and that He is available to them.[1]

We need to let our children see our prayer lives. We may pray all the time, but if our children never see us pray it can hinder their learning process. Children are always watching us, and our actions often have a much more profound effect upon their lives even than the words we speak.

What an awesome responsibility and privilege we have — to teach, train, and mentor the next generation in prayer. This is obviously one of the most important roles of parents, teachers, and church leaders. God constantly admonished Israel to teach His ways to their offspring, to instruct them in His statutes, and to pass down the stories of His faithfulness (see Psalm 78:2-7). Here are seven concepts you can use to train the children in your life to grow in their experience of prayer:

1. EMPHASIZE THAT PRAYER IS A RELATIONSHIP WITH GOD

Dear God,

What do you do with families that don't have much faith? There's a family on the next block like that. I don't want to get them in trouble. I don't want to say who. See you in church. Alexis (age 9)[2]

We often smile at the innocent prayers of children, some of them quite nonreligious. But that's the way we want them to pray — to do what they do naturally. We want them to grow up with a simple approach to prayer, having natural conversations with God.

What would a child watching your prayer life learn? If children see us praying in dull, repetitive ways, they'll get a picture of prayer opposite of what we want them to see. How will they ever see prayer as exciting? But if we pray from the heart, kids will see the freshness and power of our relationship with God.

2. TEACH GOD'S ATTRIBUTES

It's not nearly so important to teach children the mechanics of prayer as it is to help them get to know the person to whom they are praying. The more children understand who God is, the more intimately and confidently they can pray.

One way you can help children grow in their knowledge of who their heavenly Father is and what He's like is to have them make a notebook on the attributes of God. Susan Lingo suggests this idea in her book *Teaching Our Children to Pray*. Each page can feature one letter of the alphabet along with a corresponding Scripture verse. Encourage each child to write in original words that correspond with that letter of the alphabet the truths he or she is discovering about God. You might ask the child to write "favorite things" about the heavenly Father or illustrate them through drawings.[3]

When Nicole was a little girl I helped her learn more about God by teaching her the Lord's Prayer. This was not so much a matter of her *memorizing* the prayer as it was her learning to use it as a *model* for prayer. I would sit beside her and talk to her about the Lord and how faithful He had been to our family. Sometimes I would lay my hand on her head and sing or speak prayers over her life. These often centered on how much God loved her and how precious she was to Him. As Nicole grew a little older, I invited her to engage in the prayer time—to be my prayer partner. Since I was using the Lord's Prayer as a model in my personal prayer life at that time, we used each phrase of the prayer to guide us.

When we prayed, "Our Father which art in heaven . . ." I stopped and talked about how we relate to God as "Abba" or daddy. Some children may not have had good experiences with their biological dads, so it's important to say something like, "Your heavenly Father is even better than your own dad because God never makes mistakes and His love for you is perfect."

When we prayed, "Hallowed be thy name," I explained that God has different names and each one tells us something special about who He is. When we approach Him as Jehovah-Shalom, our peace, we can ask the Lord to settle our hearts in any troubling circumstances we were facing. When we come to Him as Jehovah-Rapha, our healer, then we take our physical and emotional pains to Him. Nicole learned that Jehovah-Jireh is her provider and that she can ask Him to meet her needs. As we continued through the Lord's Prayer, it gave us the opportunity to discuss that God forgives our sins, strengthens us to resist temptation, protects us from the Evil One, and more.

3. TEACH CHILDREN TO PRAY GOD'S WORD

Many children (and adults, for that matter) never mature in their prayer lives because they lack a prayer vocabulary. However, when we use Scripture to help us formulate our prayers, a whole new way of talking to God opens up to us — new words, new concepts, and new things to pray about. For example, we might ask God to grant us a spirit of wisdom and revelation (see Ephesians 1:17). Or a child might pray to grow in wisdom and stature, and favor with God and men (see Luke 2:52). A child with God's Word planted deeply in the heart and an understanding of the concept of praying Scripture is equipped to pray in the varied circumstances of life he or she will face.

For months when Nicole was about five, I had been diligently trying to teach her to pray God's Word. Then one Sunday following the church service, I noticed that Nicole had cornered our pastor and was having what seemed like a serious conversation. I later learned that she had been asking him if she could sing a solo in church.

Later that week the pastor approached us to say that he would, in fact, like for Nicole to sing a solo. As she sat beside us the next Sunday morning waiting to be called up, I felt sure that I was the only one with butterflies in my stomach. But a few moments later, I felt a little hand grab mine.

"Mommy, will you pray with me?" she asked.

"Of course, honey!" I responded.

"Just agree with me while I pray," she said.

Then she began to quote a Scripture—one that I had never even taught her: "When I am afraid, I will trust in you" (Psalm 56:3). She said, "I'll be all right now."

Moments later, with fifty kids gathered around her and the eyes of five hundred adults set upon her, Nicole stood on the platform, poised and confident, singing, "Lord, Make Me a Servant." It was as much a testimony to me as it was to Nicole that praying God's Word releases tremendous power.

4. TRAIN THEIR EARS TO HEAR GOD'S VOICE

"But how can we hear God?" children often ask. "Do we hear Him in the same way we hear Mom calling us to dinner?"

Dick Eastman explains it this way:

> *Usually, hearing God means that our hearts receive an idea from Him. Here's an example: I can point to the sky and say out loud, "The sky is blue." But I can also close my eyes and say silently in my mind, The sky is blue. To me, the words said in my mind are just as clear as those spoken out loud. They are real words, even though my ears can't hear them. When we hear like this from God, it is called the "still small voice of God."*[4]

Children need to know that God wants to talk to them. We must help children learn to listen to God, to become comfortable with silence in prayer. Jesus says, "I am the Good Shepherd, and my sheep know my voice" (see John 10:14,27).

Jocelyn Shover shares how she had an exciting experience learning to listen to the Holy Spirit when she was only nine years old. One night at bedtime while Jocelyn and her parents were praying together, they began to discuss the need not only to ask God for things but also to take time to listen to Him. Shortly after Jocelyn quieted her heart, she felt God tell her their family was going to adopt a little girl and name her Bethany.

A year later while her parents were visiting Thailand, Jocelyn's mom heard the Lord tell her that she and her husband were to adopt a little girl from that country. Many adoption obstacles followed; however, three and a half years after Jocelyn heard the Holy Spirit in prayer, the Shovers welcomed a new daughter into their home. Her name? Bethany, of course.[5]

Victory Christian Center in Tulsa, Oklahoma, has formed children's prayer teams so that kids can minister to kids during Vacation Bible School. One day the Spirit of God spoke to a girl on the prayer team that He wanted her to pray during the ministry time for a boy named Justin. She didn't know anyone named Justin, but she offered her assistance and ended up praying for a boy who wanted to accept Jesus. He also had some sins he wanted to confess. After reading 1 John 1:9 to him, she prayed for him to receive Jesus. After the prayer time was over, the boy told her his name was Justin.[6]

One big reason kids need to learn to hear God's voice is because someday it may save their lives! I regularly tell children and teenagers that God wants to warn them of impending danger. If they will tune their ears to hear His voice, He'll guide their steps out of harm's way.

Doug and Arlyn are grateful that their daughter Heather learned to hear God's voice at an early age and has continued to make listening to God a part of her lifestyle. One Sunday morning, on her way to church, Heather was driving alone on the freeway. She was following behind a truck and trailer when she felt a distinct impression that she should change lanes. Immediately Heather obeyed the prompting in her spirit, and within a split second the trailer came loose from the truck that was towing it, quickly intersecting the very spot where Heather had been driving. Even in the other lane, Heather narrowly missed colliding with the trailer as it slammed into the median. Thankfully, no one was injured. Heather pulled off the freeway and stopped her car long enough to gather her composure and thank the Lord for speaking to her to change lanes at just the right time. Hearing God's voice saved her life!

5. SHARE THAT GOD RESPONDS TO SIMPLE FAITH

One of the best ways to instill faith in children is to share with them the faithfulness of God. When parents, teachers, and church workers tell children their most memorable faith stories, it is usually not long before the children start having faith stories of their own.

While we were living on a shoestring budget working in full-time ministry, our daughter grew up hearing the stories of how God had faithfully met our needs. She has heard our stories of answered prayer regarding provision for groceries, house payments, Christian school tuition, automobiles, and airline tickets. Through this she has learned to trust God for personal needs, including Easter dresses, money for mission trips, and the healing of stomach problems, as well as broken hearts.

Hal and I taught her what the Bible says about the connection between faith and answered prayer. Nicole knows many verses by heart, such as, "This is the confidence we have in approaching God: that if we ask anything according to his will, he hears us. And if we know that he hears us — whatever we ask — we know that we have what we asked of him" (1 John 5:14-15). She quotes, "Whatever you ask for in prayer, believe that you have received it, and it will be yours" (Mark 11:24). This faith principle is much easier for children to grasp than for adults.

As a result, in more than one instance, Nicole has taught us about childlike faith rather than vice versa. I remember vividly how Nicole began to beg me to let her take piano lessons when she was quite young. At the time we did not own a piano and did not have the money for her even to take lessons. Finally, after several months I called a piano teacher and set up her first lesson. God miraculously provided for the first week's payment, and Nicole went to a neighbor's house to practice her lessons.

This scenario continued for about four weeks until one day Nicole approached me. "I thought God wanted me to take piano lessons," she said. "But He hasn't given me a piano."

"I know, honey," I responded.

"Well, what do you think about praying like this?" she asked. "God, if You want me to take piano lessons, then I need for You to give me a piano. If You don't bring me a piano then I will take that to mean You don't want me to take lessons."

"That's really putting God on the spot," I said. "Although I've never prayed that way, it sounds okay."

By the end of the week we had received a call from some friends asking if we could take a piano off their hands. The piano was nearly a hundred years old, with a cracked soundboard, yet was perfect for a beginning piano student.

Two years later Nicole was bemoaning the fact that some of the keys on her piano didn't work. She insisted that if she was to continue lessons she would need a better piano.

"You'll have to get a new piano the same way you got the last one," I told her.

She prayed again, and six weeks later her Aunt Freddi shipped her an almost new piano—her aunt decided she would probably never take the time to learn to play it, so why not give it away?

A couple of months later Nicole came home from school and announced that her Brownie camp was scheduled to be held the same week as her piano recital. "May I miss my piano recital?" she asked.

Like any responsible parent, I replied, "No way!"

"Well, would you pray with me that the date of the piano recital will be changed?" she persisted.

"No way!" I asserted firmly. "God is not going to change the date of your piano recital! The recital is only one week away, and you know how difficult it is for your teacher to find a date that works for the schedules of fifteen different families. You are simply going to have to miss Brownie camp."

The next morning as she was getting dressed for school, Nicole let me know in no uncertain terms that my words of unbelief had "dashed her faith." However she felt she could muster up enough faith to pray without me and perhaps she could get her dad to agree with her in prayer on the way to school.

It was all I could do to keep from laughing. I was still laughing when the phone rang at 9:30 that very morning. It was Debbie, Nicole's piano teacher. "I'm terribly sorry," she said, "but I'm going to have to reschedule the piano recital this weekend!"

That day Nicole taught me something about childlike faith. And I learned that God would move heaven and earth if necessary in response to the faith-filled prayers of a little child!

6. TEACH CHILDREN TO HANDLE DISAPPOINTMENT IN PRAYER

This may seem contrary to my previous point: Sometimes God doesn't respond to our prayers in the time or way we feel He should. It is important for children to develop a relationship with

God that goes beyond expecting to receive everything requested in prayer.

For various reasons, God sometimes doesn't answer our prayers in the way we've asked. Perhaps the request is not within His will. Other times we waver in our faith. Sometimes we ask with wrong motives, or there is some other sin in our lives. Other times our prayers are not answered immediately because our request is not within God's timing.

Children ask questions, and, whenever possible, we need to give them answers. However, we must guard against giving pat answers. Sometimes there will be no satisfactory answer to give.

When our sixteen-year-old friend Matthew Buckley drowned in the Salt River a few years ago, we prayed for a miracle—yet the miracle we were trusting God for didn't come. Our family and the entire Faith Life Academy attended the funeral. We wept a lot, and we all asked God a lot of questions. The bottom line is that no matter what happens, keep trusting God. He is faithful. This is where our actions as parents and teachers speak louder than words. In times of crisis and disappointment, children watch to see if we really believe what we teach.

7. HELP CHILDREN RECEIVE AND GIVE THE PRAYER OF SALVATION

Hopefully, one of the first prayers a child learns is the one he or she can pray to receive Jesus Christ as personal Savior. The child must have a real encounter with the living God so that his or her life will be spiritually transformed. Praying in original words or being led in a prayer by someone else, the child must believe in his heart and confess with his mouth that Jesus is Lord.

Later it is important that the child learns the importance of praying for others to come to Christ, including how to lead someone else in the prayer of salvation. Here is a model prayer for leading a child to Christ. It is also a good prayer for children to memorize so they are prepared to lead someone else to Christ.

Dear Father in heaven, today I give my life to You. Please forgive me for all the things I've done wrong and wash me clean. I believe that Jesus is Your Son and that He paid for my sins with His blood on the cross. I ask You, Jesus, to come into my heart and save me. Thank You for hearing my prayer and for forgiving me. I know that I am now a Christian. When I die I get to go to heaven and live forever with Jesus. For now, I have You living with me every day. You are my best friend. Thank You, Lord, for saving me. Amen.

TAKE IT OUT OF THE HOUSE

To teach children the attributes of God, children's ministry leaders Mike and Dottie Steczo have set up some forty unique prayer stations in the Sunday school halls at their church in Colorado Springs, Colorado. The focus of each station is a simple rectangle painted on the wall in a different color. At the top of each is a name of God or one of His characteristics (such as "He is our Father," "God is our Protector," "Jesus is the Rock," "He is our Salvation"). Within each rectangle are Scriptures and prayers that describe each name or attribute.

Families in the church are encouraged to adopt a prayer station that means something special to them. Families seal their adoption by leaving brightly colored handprints all around the station they selected. As families walk down the halls, they can meditate on the names of God, discuss the truth of the characteristics, read the Scriptures, and pray for whomever God puts on their hearts — their family, lost friends, the nation, or children of the world. The church also has produced kids' prayer journals that correspond to the prayer stations. And the prayer stations have become so popular that many families have reproduced them at home by using poster board, felt-tip pens, and photos.[7]

SATURATE YOUR CHILD IN PRAYER TODAY

Dear Heavenly Father, I lift _____ before You today. I pray that _____ will learn the importance of spending focused time with You every day. Please give me wisdom to train my child in the ministry of intercession. Bring others across _____'s pathway, those he/she will look up to, who will model a life of prayer. May _____ learn to pray with passion and power, to do battle against the Enemy, and to hear Your voice. May the course of history be changed because of _____'s life of intercession. I pray this in Jesus's name—the name that is above every name. Amen.

CHAPTER 7

FURTHER UP AND FURTHER IN

No eye has seen, no ear has heard, and no mind has imagined what God has prepared for those who love him. But it was to us that God revealed these things by his Spirit. For his Spirit searches out everything and shows us God's deep secrets. (1 Corinthians 2:9-10, NLT)

"Quick," said Peter, "there's nowhere else to hide!" Flinging open the wardrobe, he jumped in—with Susan, Edmund, and Lucy close behind. Bundled inside the closet the four children burrowed among the coats, their faces brushing against the fur as they made their way to the back. As they went farther in they found a second row of coats hanging behind the first. Pushing their way through, the children took two steps, then three. *It was surprising how much room was inside!*

Suddenly they found themselves walking not through coats but through something hard and rough and even prickly. Why, it felt just like tree branches! The temperature was dropping rapidly, and at the same time the children felt something cold and crunchy under their feet. Then they saw a light ahead—and a moment later found themselves standing in the middle of a snowy wood. Behind them stood the open door to the wardrobe. They could practically see the empty room on the other side. Yet on this side of the wardrobe the children had entered another country—a strange and wonderful world where they were about to encounter a myriad of intriguing adventures and fierce battles.

The children in the CHRONICLES OF NARNIA series by C. S. Lewis learned with each new adventure and battle that the "further up and further in" you go, *the bigger everything gets*! As Peter, Susan, Edmund, and Lucy discovered when they stepped into the wardrobe, the inside was larger than the outside.[1]

So it is with prayer.

THE MEANING AND MYSTERY OF THE PRAYER CLOSET

The time comes when it's not enough just to pray *for* and *with* our children. They must develop their own personal relationships with the Lord. You may want to introduce the concept of a quiet time with God by talking with children about the meaning and mystery of the prayer closet.

Jesus talks about a special place for prayer in Matthew 6:6. The *King James Version* calls it a prayer "closet"; the *New International Version* describes a room where you can close the door. It represents a quiet place where we meet with God—to talk to Him, to worship Him, to read His Word, to hear what He has to say to us. This may be a literal closet or room, or it may be another special place such as a favorite chair, a park bench, or under a tree.

You might introduce your child to the idea of a prayer closet by discussing various types of closets. For example, bedroom closets contain clothes and shoes. Bathroom closets hold towels and linens while hall closets keep old pictures and many memories.

Ask your child, "What are some things we might find in a prayer closet?" Suggest such things as a Bible, pictures of people you are praying for, worship music, and paper and pencil for journaling prayer requests and things God speaks to your heart.

Most importantly, a prayer closet is a place where we can enjoy the things of God. These things are very real although we can't see them with our eyes. They include friendship with God, the voice of the Holy Spirit, the armor of God, and power to accomplish God's mission for us on the earth.

Though prayer closets are quite different from other kinds of closets, they are similar in one way. Just as other kinds of closets keep our belongings organized, spending time in the prayer closet keeps our lives clean and in order. In the prayer closet we learn to put first things first. There we find purpose and direction for our lives.

Sometimes we need to clean the junk out of our closets. In the prayer closet, however, God will clean the junk out of *us*. We may enter with guilt and shame or a big problem for which we have no answer. When we take these things to Jesus, we can leave feeling clean and at peace. Encourage your children to think about an imaginary shelf in their prayer closet where they leave all of their sorrows, sin, and burdens with God.[2]

Perhaps the psalmist David had a prayer closet in mind when he wrote, "You are my hiding place; you will protect me from trouble and surround me with songs of deliverance" (Psalm 32:7).

The wonder and mystery of the prayer closet is this: No matter how far up and how far in you go, there is always more to see. Just as we reach the pinnacle of our mountain's climb, we discover a whole new land stretched out before us—all beckoning exploration and filled with endless spiritual adventures. Children are intrigued by adventure. They like action. That's what they're looking for in their Christianity. They don't want to just hear about heroes of the faith, they want to have adventures themselves. They say, "Don't just teach me about David and Goliath. I want to slay a few giants of my own!"

CHILDREN AND ADVENTURES WITH THE HOLY SPIRIT

Children are hungry for supernatural experiences such as those they hear about in the Bible. Many times children are well-acquainted with God the Father and Jesus the Son, yet have not had much teaching about or experience with the Holy Spirit. The Holy Spirit is the person of the Godhead who is in charge of the supernatural here on earth. All we have to do is ask, and He will come.

Nowhere in the Bible do we find that supernatural adventures are reserved for people over twenty-one. In fact, God *promises* that He will pour out His Spirit upon our children and youth: "And afterward, I will pour out my Spirit on all people. Your sons and daughters will prophesy, your old men will dream dreams, your young men will see visions" (Joel 2:28-29).

My (Cheryl's) daughter Nicole became acquainted with the Holy Spirit when she was quite young. After that, supernatural experiences were commonplace in her life.

One such instance happened on the last day of a family vacation in Rocky Point, Mexico. We had just finished packing the car and were preparing to leave our summer getaway when Hal noticed that the car was out of gas. Leaving Nicole and me behind, he borrowed one of the ATVs from the garage and took off for the nearest gas station.

One hour went by, then two, then three. When the sun began to go down I started to worry. "I think we'd better pray for your dad," I told Nicole.

We hadn't prayed long when Nicole said, "Mom, I think Dad

is stuck in the mud somewhere."

"I'm sure he's okay," I tried to comfort her.

"No, he's not!" she insisted. "Dad is stuck in the 'miry clay.' The Lord just showed me a picture of him in some swamp." We both remembered the verse in Psalm 40:2, KJV: "He brought me up also out of an horrible pit, out of the miry clay, and set my feet upon a rock, and established my goings." So we prayed that's just what the Lord would do. Soon after, Hal returned—covered in mud from head to toe. He explained that he'd decided to take a shortcut across what looked like a dry, barren area—only to discover that under the crusty top was a muddy swamp. He had to walk into town and pay a tow truck to rescue the ATV.

The Holy Spirit may come to us or our children in ways that surprise us! You might ask children these questions to open up the subject:

- Have you ever experienced a time when you were praying for someone and you felt like you needed to cry for him or her?
- Have you ever seen a picture in your head of a need someone had or a picture of what was happening while you were praying?
- Were you surprised when these things happened? Did you pray? What kinds of things resulted?[3]

Children may experience adventures with the Holy Spirit in the following ways, among others.

DREAMS

Sometimes God uses dreams to speak to us about a circumstance that needs prayer. It's important to explain to children that God doesn't want bad things to happen to them. So if a child has a dream in which something bad happens to someone, then encourage him or her to pray about it. The Enemy may have been trying to scare the child, or God may have been calling the child to intercede and prevent a bad situation from occurring. We shouldn't make a big deal about every dream a child has, yet it's important to help children realize that God can use dreams to talk to them.

FASTING

We often think of fasting as something that only adults can do. Yet fasting is a spiritual discipline we need to teach our children. When we quiet our minds and lives and give up natural desires, we increase our spiritual appetite and can hear God's voice more clearly. We would not necessarily want to encourage young children to skip a meal. However they can fast from desserts, soda, television, video games, or some other activity. Encourage them to devote time to prayer and Bible reading in place of these activities.

PRAYERWALKING

One of the most exciting spiritual adventures children can undertake is prayerwalking. It's praying in the very places where we expect God to answer—such as neighborhoods, schools, churches, businesses, and government buildings. As author Steve Hawthorne points out, prayerwalking isn't just about walking around or praying outside. It's getting nearer to pray clearer.[4] The next time your family goes on a walk together, why not pray for the people you see and the homes and buildings you pass?

Arlyn's family prayerwalked their neighborhood regularly for months and saw two families come to Christ—parents and children. One of these families went on some prayerwalks with Arlyn's family to join in praying for the neighborhood, and even more remarkable things began to happen. They passed an empty house and prayed that God would fill it with a Christian family. And guess what? God did!

As you prepare to prayerwalk with your children, you may

want to show them pictures of schools and other places in the neighborhood where you plan to go. Give your children opportunity to pray for the things they see and the places they go. Upon returning, ask the children to talk about what they saw. Let them talk about things that they observed, such as the condition of the neighborhood, people they saw, and what they think was on Jesus' heart for the people who lived there.

SPIRITUAL BATTLES

We've heard some parents and Christian leaders advise against teaching children about spiritual warfare and the Devil. They say that doing so may frighten children. We disagree.

In a world filled with domestic violence, school shootings, and terrorist attacks, most children are well aware that the world is a dangerous place. To release children into the world without an understanding of who their enemy is—and the authority they have in Christ—is like sending them to war without weapons.

In addition to facing threats to their physical well-being, children today are engaged in a battle for their minds and souls. Just take one look in the children's department of bookstores, the comic book section of grocery stores, movies, Saturday morning cartoons, and, I'm sorry to say, even the curricula in our schools. You'll discover evidence of Satan's trap strategically set to ensnare our children in the dark side of the supernatural—witches, warlocks, ghosts, and every strain of the occult, including voodoo and devil worship. We must make sure that our children are filled with the *Holy Spirit* lest they become tempted to fill their spiritual hunger for the supernatural with an *unholy* spirit.

Taking Authority

If children are to be successful in spiritual battle, they need to know who God is, who their enemy is, and how to take the authority they have in Christ. Reassure children that God has already won the war with Satan, because God is more powerful. And because of Jesus' death on the cross to pay the penalty for sin, Christians—even kids—are guaranteed victory over the Devil. Taking authority simply means commanding, out loud, any actual or potential activity of the Enemy to be shut down, as seen in Matthew 4:10; Luke 10:19; Acts 16:18; James 4:7; and 1 Peter 5:9.

One way to demonstrate spiritual authority to kids is by comparing it to being knighted. Children may be familiar with the ancient British custom of knighting someone. When a person was knighted, authority was conferred on him to fight in the king's name, as well as the honor of being known as a soldier in the king's service (see Philippians 2:25; 2 Timothy 2:3; Philemon 1:2).

To illustrate this, you may want to hold a knighting ceremony. Gather the kids in a circle. If you have a toy sword, you can "knight" each child (touch him or her lightly on each shoulder with the flat of the sword). You can say something like, "Kevin, because of your faith in Jesus, you are a soldier of Jesus Christ. Jesus has given you authority to fight in His name and to have victory over the power of the Enemy. Be strong and courageous!" Repeat with each child, inserting the appropriate name. Then give kids the opportunity to thank God for the privilege of serving in His army. Remind them to thank God also that He gives them power over the Enemy's tricks when they fight back in Jesus' name.[5]

Ten-year-old Allyson learned to use Christ's authority over spiritual battles she was facing when she struggled with feelings of fear and loneliness. She often felt that nobody loved her, not even her parents. At school, sometimes the other girls would have clubs and would exclude Allyson. Or they would let her in for a while and then vote her out. Allyson often had dreams that frightened her. When she awoke she cried and felt scared and lonely.

After a while Allyson began to realize that she was in a battle — but not with people. She was in a fight with the Enemy, who is a spirit. This was spiritual warfare, and Allyson knew she had to fight back.

She asked Jesus to help her. She remembered that the Bible says, "God did not give us a spirit of timidity, but a spirit of power, of love and of self-discipline" (2 Timothy 1:7). So she asked Jesus to give her power and love and to take away the fear and feelings of being unloved. She commanded the Enemy to go away in Jesus' name and to stop trying to make her feel fearful, sad, and alone. The Lord always made her feel stronger and reminded her of how much He loves her.

When the feelings return, Allyson knows what to do: "I pray — right out loud! The Enemy has to listen to Jesus, and Jesus lives in me!"[6]

PRAYING FOR OUR ENEMIES

As a former schoolteacher, I've seen firsthand how cruel children can be to one another. Whether it's being left out of a clique, persecuted for being different, or bullied for no reason at all, school children often feel like grasshoppers in the land of giants. Dealing with rejection from friends and classmates can be one of the biggest battles children and youth face. Equipping them to pray and respond in a Christlike manner toward their enemies is one of the most important weapons of war we can put in their hands.

I heard of one little girl back in the sixties who encountered unimaginable persecution in her own community. As she walked home from school, frenzied people lined the streets, screaming, cursing, and threatening to kill her.

Why? Because Ruby Bridges was black, the first black child to attend that all-white school. And in New Orleans in 1960, enough people hated the idea of black and white children sitting in the same classroom that Ruby needed protection from the daily barrage of hate.

You'd think that Ruby and her family might bow under the pressure. Even if she didn't quit school, surely she would become depressed and frightened. But she didn't. Ruby was cheerful, happy to be in the school. Even her teacher couldn't understand it.

"You know, I don't understand this child," the teacher told Robert Coles, a psychiatrist who was watching Ruby to see how she handled the pressure. "She seems so happy."

Dr. Coles didn't understand it either. Surely there was something wrong with Ruby that she just wasn't showing. She couldn't possibly be as cheerful as she appeared.

One day Ruby's teacher saw her stop outside the school and talk to the crowd. Startled, the teacher mentioned it to Dr. Coles.

That night, Coles went to Ruby's home to find out what had happened. "Ruby," he said, "your teacher told me she saw you talking to those people outside the school today."

"Oh, I wasn't talking to them," Ruby answered, "I was just saying a prayer for them."

Every day, Ruby and her family prayed for those screaming people. Why? "Because," Ruby explained, "they needed praying for." [7]

Our children will probably never encounter the severity of opposition and persecution that Ruby did, but we can still equip them to respond to their enemies in the same way she did. The sword of the Spirit, God's Word, is a powerful weapon in warfare. Jesus commanded: "Love your enemies and pray for those who persecute you" (Matthew 5:44).

BREAKING CURSES

One of my good friends confided recently that her son came home from school and announced, "Did you know Josh and his mom are Wiccan?" My friend was astounded. She had no idea her son was exposed to things like the religion of Wicca or witchcraft. Kids today are exposed to the occult on a regular basis at school, the mall, movie theaters, and even in the homes of their friends. In junior highs and high schools today it is becoming quite popular for kids to embrace Wiccan beliefs just as casually as they might embrace any other religion.

Involvement in the occult is not a harmless pastime. It is dangerous involvement with the dark side of the supernatural. Your child's friends or their friends' siblings or parents may be speaking or "praying" curses over them. A curse is quite simply "an appeal to a supernatural power for evil or injury to befall someone or something."[8] Unknowingly, your child may be subjected to the influence of demonic spirits and accompanying curses. So it's important to pray protection over your children regularly, breaking any word curses over them and closing occult doors in Jesus' name. Children who are old enough to understand can learn to pray protection over themselves from such things. The Bible warns us not to be ignorant of Satan's schemes, "that [he] might not outwit us" (2 Corinthians 2:11).

In our naturalistic society we often do not give credence to the reality of the supernatural (much less curses), but it is all too real—and increasingly so as occult involvement is on the rise. With more and more kids getting involved in Wicca, role-playing games such as Dungeons and Dragons or Magic: The Gathering, heavy metal music, Ouija boards, and other "games," it is very likely that your child will encounter a curse at some time or another.

While "cursing" was well understood in biblical cultures (and still is in many other cultures today), in Western culture we underestimate the power of words spoken with purposeful intent and conviction. But as we pointed out in chapter 4, spoken words *do* have power—for good and for evil—with lasting results.

God's Word gives us both a promise and a commandment for dealing with curses. The promise is "Like a fluttering sparrow or a darting swallow, an undeserved curse does not come to rest" (Proverbs 26:2). Jesus commanded, "Bless those who curse you, pray for those who mistreat you" (Luke 6:28). When you become aware or even suspicious that there may be curses being spoken against your child, prayers of protection (for your child) and forgiveness and blessing (for the offender) are in order. Identify any known curses and declare God's protection over your child. Pray for His blessing to be poured out. Forgive the one who has uttered curses against your child and pray for God's blessing to come to that person, especially the blessing of salvation.[9] If the child is aware of an action that has brought him into contact with a curse, he should confess any known wrongdoing and verbally break any curses he may have encountered.

Our kids aren't immune to the presence of evil in this world, yet they need not be overcome by it. "Do not be overcome by evil, but overcome evil with good," the apostle Paul exhorted his readers who were living in the pagan culture of Rome (Romans 12:21).

In the CHRONICLES OF NARNIA series, Aslan gave the Pevensie children special gifts to help them overcome the obstacles they would encounter in their adventures and battles. Our kids have been given special gifts, too—by Jesus—to protect, equip, and empower them. As with any adventure, there will certainly be dangers, enemies, and both human and spiritual opposition along life's way. Our children need to know they are armed with the knowledge that they are "more than conquerors through him who loved us" (Romans 8:37)!

TAKE IT OUT OF THE HOUSE

During Sunday school or a children's prayer ministry time, set up a prayer closet in your classroom—perhaps a large refrigerator box with a door and windows cut in it to give some light. Or ask a craftsman in your church to make a closet out of wood. Another possibility is to set up a quiet corner in the room separated by portable panels or curtains. Let children place in the prayer closet items such as pillows, blankets, Bibles, and Scripture verses to facilitate times of prayer. One or two children at a time may go into the prayer closet at appropriate times during the class period. They may enjoy it so much that they'll want to create a prayer closet of their own at home!

SATURATE YOUR CHILD WITH PRAYER TODAY

Dear Heavenly Father, I pray that _____ *will come to know You as Father and Jesus as Lord. Fill* _____ *with the power of Your Holy Spirit. May* _____ *be open to receive all Your spiritual gifts, Your power to fulfill his (or her) God-given calling, and Your strength to overcome every internal and external obstacle. Lord, please take* _____ *on a spiritual adventure and help* _____ *accomplish great things for Your kingdom. Give* _____ *a spirit of wisdom and revelation into the mysteries and secrets found in the deep and intimate knowledge of You. May* _____ *walk in the center of Your perfect will all the days of his (or her) life and never veer from the path You have laid out for him (or her). Take my child further up and further in with You. I pray these things in the name of Jesus Christ, Your Son. Amen.*

CHAPTER 8

THE ROLE OF THE CHURCH

Blow the ram's horn in Jerusalem! Announce a time
of fasting; call the people together for a solemn meeting. Gather all the people—the elders, the children,
and even the babies. (Joel 2:15-16, NLT)

The line starts forming before 6:00 p.m. Parents holding the hands
of young children, and some children alone, are huddled on the
sidewalk between a squarish, plain-faced brick facade and noisy
Flatbush Avenue. By 6:30 everybody who is likely to get inside is in
line, still waiting for the doors to open. But New Yorkers are used to
that, even at church. And especially at the Brooklyn Tabernacle.

It's Tuesday night, and time for prayer meeting—the children's prayer meeting.

At 6:35 the doors open. Older children sign in and gravitate
to the walls to draw and paint on large sheets of poster board
about the night's theme. In a few minutes, the children will begin
singing, then get down to the serious business of praying for the
next two hours.

The younger children go downstairs to a basement room bright
with fluorescent lights. They start singing immediately. Prayer for

them will be interspersed with songs and stories, but this is not game time or babysitting.

"Prayer is the hub of everything we do," says Nancy Martinez, director of Christian education. "It's not tacked on to other programs. Prayer is what we're here for." [1]

NEW WINESKINS FOR CHILDREN'S MINISTRY?

"And afterward,
I will pour out my Spirit on all people.
Your sons and daughters will prophesy,
*   your old men will dream dreams,*
*   your young men will see visions." (Joel 2:28)*

God is poised to pour out His Spirit upon us and our children. In order to bring the presence of God into our children's ministries in the area of prayer, we may need to abandon some old wineskins regarding what we have always thought children's ministries should look like. What is the old wineskin? It is our own limited notions of what children are or aren't capable of spiritually.

A child who receives Jesus as Savior receives the same Holy Spirit that an adult does (see Ephesians 1:13)—not a smaller, pint-sized Holy Spirit, but the real Holy Spirit who speaks, comforts, heals, and imparts spiritual gifts. Kids today belong to a hands-on, relational, interactive generation. It's not enough for them to simply *hear* about the works of Jesus—they need to expect to *see* them in their own lives, and be taught how to do them, too!

Is it possible that we've become so focused on being wonderfully professional and entertaining that we've overlooked the more important goal of imparting spiritual life and training children to be praying, functioning disciples of Jesus Christ?

BIG CHURCH MEETS KIDS' CHURCH

One of the saddest commentaries about the value we place on children's ministry—or lack of value—is when people say they don't want to minister with children because they don't want to miss "big church"—as if what's happening in kids' church is completely devoid of any spiritual life and purpose of its own. What would our children's ministries be like if those with spiritual gifts and callings in the areas of prophecy, evangelism, teaching, and leadership made it a priority to spend at least *some* time, on a regular basis, with the children of their congregations? Some of the spiritual life and purpose that we have come to expect in our adult services would naturally begin to filter into the children's ministry as kids' workers and the kids themselves reap the blessings of the direct influence of these kinds of leaders.

Besides the practical rewards of teaching, modeling, and mentoring, there is also the huge yet often overlooked value of *impartation.* "Impart" simply means to "pass on." Spiritually speaking, we know that spiritual gifts can be "passed on"—or imparted—from leaders to those under their ministry. We know that Timothy's spiritual gifting and ministry were due, in some part, to prayers of impartation he had received from Paul (see 2 Timothy 1:6). Whether it is a spiritual gift, a word of encouragement, instruction, intercession, or moral support, everyone—including pastors, ministry leaders, elders, intercessors, and more—has something of spiritual value to contribute to children.

When Bubba Stahl was pastor of First Baptist Church in Boerne, Texas, he raised up an intercessory prayer team of ninety-seven children—all ages five to twelve—who prayed for him and the things on his heart daily. These children loved to pray for their pastor, especially when he was on mission trips. Stahl would often take his young prayer partners with him on local mission trips into their community to pray for the mayor, fire chief, or city council members. This unique pastor found a way to both mentor and release children in prayer. Stahl's greatest impact upon the church may well be the indelible imprint he leaves as a role model in the lives of the children in his congregation.[2]

At my own church, I (Arlyn) recruited a number of adult intercessors to join us one morning in FaithTREK, our children's ministry. Each intercessor was assigned to coach a group of children ranging in age from kindergarten through fifth grade. The children shared what they felt they were hearing from the Lord, then laid their hands on their teachers and prayed blessings over them. The coaches helped the children articulate what they were sensing, kept the prayer times purposeful and on track, and offered words of agreement, encouragement, and affirmation to the children as they prayed.

Nine-year-old Shannon said of her teacher, "Miss Ginger, I think God is saying you are a peacemaker and a good servant of His." Then she laid her hands on Miss Ginger's shoulder and prayed that God would bless her with His peace and strength, and that she would be happy and joyful in serving Him. As I saw group after group of praying children freely expressing their hearts to the Lord and being vessels of His love and encouragement to their teachers (and even each other, in some groups), my heart sang. *Surely this is the heart of Jesus*, I thought, *that His littlest children relate to and minister for Him in this way.*

MAKE ROOM FOR THE CHILDREN

The prayer life of children is one of the most untapped resources of the church today. We often don't take the innocent prayers of children seriously and instead send children to another room during times of corporate prayer. Jesus had a much different view of children. When the disciples attempted to keep the children from "bothering" the Master, "Jesus called the children to him and said, 'Let the little children come to me, and do not hinder them, for the kingdom of God belongs to such as these'" (Luke 18:16). Jesus made it plain that children are important to God.

Transgenerational prayer meetings are the norm at Shekinah Church in Blountville, Tennessee. Pastor Sue Curran says:

> *Our children from speaking age (two to three) know that their prayers are welcome in corporate meetings. It is not at all unusual for one or more of them to pray for me and other leaders before we preach or minister in worship services. A capacity to give themselves in prayer was developed in prayer meetings. We 'suffered the little children,' not forbidding them to come to Jesus, and as we took their prayers seriously, they became pray-ers!* [3]

We tell children that their prayers are important. However, if all we tell them during prayer time is to sit still, they get the message that prayer is only for adults.

In her book *The Prayer-Saturated Church*, Cheryl tells what happened when she and her husband, Hal, visited a church in Phoenix that included children in a Sunday morning service devoted entirely to prayer. The guest speaker, Esther Ilnisky, spoke for a few minutes then invited children and youth to join adults on the platform to help lead the prayer meeting.

"Would you pray over all the hurting and abused children in the world?" Esther asked, handing the microphone to a five-year-old boy. With stammering lips and a shaking voice the child began to pray. As he continued to pray over his hurting generation everyone was amazed at his clarity and focus.

"God, make the mothers and fathers stop fighting," he cried. "Tell them it's hurting their kids."

Then with tears streaming down his face, he fell to his knees. His little body heaved with grief. Several young children moved to pray for and comfort him as the prayer meeting continued. A young girl prayed, "God, tell the parents to stop killing our brothers and sisters through abortion." Another child prayed for the salvation of young people who did not know Christ. Others prayed for revival in their schools and that our nation would return to Christ. The simplicity of their prayers accompanied by humility and brokenness brought tremendous conviction to the hearts of the adults present.

EFFECTING A PARADIGM SHIFT

The children's ministry team at Brooklyn Tabernacle insists that understanding the spiritual capacity of kids is foundational to their children's ministry. A key verse for them is Psalm 8:2: "From the lips of children and infants you have ordained praise because of your enemies, to silence the foe and the avenger."

It's not enough to tell children Bible stories that hint about the fact that they can hear God's voice or that Jesus does heal the sick. We need to *teach* them how to listen, *instruct* them in how to do things such as lay hands on and pray for people who are ill, and *give* them opportunities to practice!

Several years ago, a Sunday school teacher named M'Linda was facing the same challenges that many children's ministers face regularly. "If I tried to get the children to pray for any length of time beyond their comfort level, they began to play and talk with their friends," she admitted.

If not every child is at the same level in a desire to pray, then how do we fill the hunger for communication with God in the few and fuel greater desire in the others?

M'Linda solved this problem by starting a children's prayer team, inviting only the kids who were genuinely interested in prayer to participate. The team met at a time other than their regular Sunday morning ministry hour. To launch the new prayer team, M'Linda sent a letter to parents of all the elementary school-age children in the church. She let them know she would be starting a prayer class for children who had a special interest or gifting in prayer. The fifty-minute class was made up of children of all elementary school ages, with the older children helping the younger ones.

In addition to starting a children's prayer team for those with a special interest in prayer, M'Linda started incorporating prayer in the existing children's ministry. By engaging children for shorter periods and with creative prayer activities, M'Linda found she could keep the children interested and excited. Here are some ideas:

TESTIMONIES

On Sunday mornings, during the first fifteen minutes of class, M'Linda invited children to share testimonies of answered prayer. One day when I (Cheryl) was visiting the class, a brother and sister told how they had been playing in the trunk of a neighbor's car earlier in the week. The trunk had been left open and the children didn't realize that if they shut the trunk, they would not be able to open it from the inside. Stuck inside, they began to pray. The boy and girl described how the Lord spoke to their mother and told her to go check on the children immediately because they were in trouble. Prayer saved their lives! M'Linda has observed that the other kids in the ministry have developed a new interest in prayer as a result of the testimonies, and passion for prayer in their children's ministry continues to grow.

PRAYER CENTERS

Becky Fischer of Kids in Ministry International in Bismarck, North Dakota, has discovered a great way to train children's prayer teams. Realizing that kids were not going to sit for an hour with their hands folded, she came up with the idea of creating prayer centers like public schools set up learning centers. When Carol Koch, copastor of a church in Lee's Summit, Missouri, heard Becky share this prayer center concept, she decided to put it into practice. Carol created one center for prayer for healing. For a visual object lesson, she obtained a first-aid kit and filled it full of adhesive bandages. In the kit, she also included a vial of anointing oil. She trains the children to pray for healing by teaching them, first of all, what the Bible says about God's healing. Then they might "practice" by anointing the Band-Aids with oil and praying for healing for someone they know who needs it.

In another center, equipped with globes and maps, the children learn to pray for the nations. Children choose one nation to pray for each week. They also have a center to pray for those who need to find salvation in Jesus Christ. Carol found a bare tree, one that had no fruit on it, and placed it in the center as an aid to interceding for the lost.

During prayer training, Carol gives the children free time to go to the center they believe God is leading them to. The children love it! They are actively learning and practicing new and powerful ways to pray.[4]

HANDS-ON PRAYER FOR ONE ANOTHER

One day I (Arlyn) was teaching and ministering with our church's elementary-age kids as they learned about—and practiced—prayers of blessing and encouragement over others. Healing prayers were not on my lesson plan, but that sure didn't stop six-year-old Devon! I watched Devon hold eight-year-old Joseph's limp feet in his hands and wiggle them. It seemed as if he wondered if, somehow, he could impart enough strength that Joseph might spring from his wheelchair to run and play with the rest of the children. Joseph's hands waved aimlessly in the air and he made guttural, unintelligible sounds. Devon shut his eyes tightly and lifted his face heavenward.

"God," he prayed earnestly, "please fix Joseph's brain so he can talk to us!"

Three other first-graders gathered behind the wheelchair and put their hands on Joseph's shoulders. They didn't say anything, but I could tell they agreed. I didn't feel that I needed to add a single thing.

How did Devon know to pray that way? As far as I knew, he wasn't accustomed to praying for healing. But after practicing prayers of encouragement for a while in his small group, Devon had looked up and spotted Joseph across the room, and he took it from there—a child's faith in action!

CHILDREN'S PRAYER CONFERENCES

When my church—Destiny City Church in Tacoma, Washington —held an adult conference over the course of several midweek evenings, our children's ministry team wanted to provide more than just child care. So each evening, through teaching, games, and prayer activities, we focused on teaching the children how to pray.

The first night we taught them how to confess their sins in prayer. I asked all the children to raise their hands and show them to me. "Are they clean?" I asked. Everyone thought so. But were they *really* clean? I pointed out to the children that there are germs on their hands, and even though we can't see them, germs can make us *sick*. Then I gave each child a squeeze of some antibacterial gel, reminding them that washing their hands cleans away the germs so they can't make us sick. I pointed out how unconfessed sin can be the same way—nobody can see it but it has the power to hurt us—and how confession, like antibacterial gel, can wipe it away.

We taped large pieces of butcher paper on all four walls of the room and wrote one of these words on each sheet: eyes, mouth, hands, and thoughts. I asked the children to be still for a moment. Then I invited the Holy Spirit to speak to their hearts about any ways they had sinned with their eyes, mouths, hands, or thoughts. Then I threw handfuls of markers into the crowd and sent them off to write their simple confessions on the walls. The children were open and honest, listing things like "being angry," "pushing my brother," "calling my sister names," and "arguing with my mom."

After a time, all the children came back together to the center of the room so they could "get their hands clean." I talked with them about 1 John 1:9—about how when we confess our sin, Jesus is faithful to forgive us and make us clean. Then I asked them to hold out their hands to God and led them in a repeat-after-me corporate confession in which I gave them the opportunity to call out the things they had written on the butcher paper. And they did!

Those kids didn't just learn *about* confession. They really learned to *do* it![5]

The bottom line is that we don't want to give kids another lesson, another video, or another puppet show—as well-intended and entertaining as those things may be. We want to give them hands-on opportunities to do what they are being taught (and in some cases have been taught for years).

TRAINING PARENTS

Few parents feel adequate to train their children spiritually without any assistance. They are seeking instruction, resources, and encouragement to help them along the way. For this they look to their local church.

George Barna says,

> *Parents across the nation admit one of the greatest benefits*
> *they receive from attending church is having that community*

of faith assume responsibility for the spiritual development of their children. Knowing that there are trained professionals and other willing individuals who will provide spiritual guidance to their children is a source of security and comfort for most churchgoing adults.[6]

One children's minister at Cheryl's church (Word of Grace Church in Mesa, Arizona) decided to hold a two-hour seminar to help parents learn to pray for their toddlers. When parents came to pick up their children after church one Sunday, she handed each one a brightly colored flyer. It read: "Have You Prayed for Your Children Today? If you would like to learn more about how to pray for your children come to room C102 Wednesday evening from 7:00 to 9:00 p.m. We're holding a special seminar just for you!"

The *PrayKids! Teacher's Guide: A Hands-On Guide for Developing Kids Who Pray* (NavPress) is a great resource tool for ministry leaders and parents who want to help their children and their parents grow in all areas of prayer. When my church was using the *Pray*Kids! prayer curriculum, I invited parents to work with their children at home by accessing the *Pray*Kids! website and following along with the lessons on intercession, petition, spiritual warfare, authority, and more. Parents were eager to use the material to stimulate their own family prayer times, and I know some parents were learning right along with their children![7]

TRAINING CHILDREN'S MINISTERS

I (Arlyn) love to see the purple-shirted children's ministers at my own church gather for prayer in their classrooms every Sunday. Sometimes their arms are wrapped around each other's shoulders as they seek God's presence and power for the children that day. They intercede for specific children. They ask God to expose schemes of the Enemy against the children and the ministry time so they can dismantle and avert them through spiritual warfare prayer. Sometimes they lay hands on the teacher and pray for God to speak through him or her. Oftentimes the children see their leaders praying like this as they come into class and join in. As a parent, I feel secure and privileged in placing my children under this spiritual leadership because I know they are seeking God themselves as they help my children to hear from and follow Him, as well.

The best way to train children's ministers is to model for them what you want them to do. Pray with them, for them, and over them. It is vital in this process that the children's ministry leader be committed to prayer and a cheerleader for the children's efforts and spiritual capacities. It's also important to have a children's ministry team that is tracking with this paradigm. If you're a parent, talk to leadership about some of these ideas. If you're a leader in your church, you can help to bring about some important opportunities:

- Hold monthly or quarterly meetings that include instruction about training and equipping children in prayer.
- Bring in your church's prayer ministry team and ask them to pray over your children's ministers on a regular basis.
- Encourage your children's ministry team to attend prayer conferences. Have a debriefing afterward to discuss and pray about how to apply what they learned to children's ministry.
- Recommend good books on prayer and children's ministry. Consider reading through one together at the same time. Provide thought and/or discussion questions to help the team make direct application to their own ministry.
- Make sure children's ministers have time off to be fed and

nurtured by what is being shared and experienced in the larger congregation so that they can come back with fresh vision, enthusiasm, and power. Regularly cross-pollinate your teams with new members, especially seeking out people who are strong in prayer.

RAISING UP A CHILDREN'S PRAYER SHIELD

Whatever methods and resources you use, it is important to make certain that the children of your church are covered in prayer. A wonderful goal is for every child in the church to be adopted in prayer by a mature Christian intercessor. Because of children's inexperience, vulnerability, physical limitations, temptations, and spiritual warfare, it is important that someone is praying for every child in your church daily.

Some youth pastors and church prayer coordinators set aside one service a year for the church body to pray for the younger generation. A good time to do this is in August when families are focusing on the beginning of a new school year. When Kurt Cotter was the youth pastor at Living Streams Christian Church in Phoenix, Arizona, he planned what turned out to be an effective and dynamic youth service. Here's what he says,

> *In response to the prompting of the Holy Spirit, I took our regularly scheduled youth Sunday to preach to our congregation about the principles of intercessory prayer and the need for our church family to raise up a prayer covering for our youth.*
>
> *The young people in our youth department conducted every part of the service, except for my sermon. They served as ushers, received the offering, led praise and worship. Others shared their testimonies or gave short exhortations from the Scriptures.*
>
> *At the close of the service, we called the young people to*

the front of the church and challenged the adult members of the congregation to consider adopting a youth in prayer for a year. I exhorted them, "Will you ask God to protect the youth for whom you are praying? To draw him or her away from ungodly influences? To give him or her a heart to follow after the things of God and to fulfill his or her destiny in Christ?"

In preparation for this special service, we had taken photos of everyone involved in our youth group. We also compiled a three-by-five card of basic biographical information on each student to help an intercessor pray more effectively. The students passed out the photos and biographical information to each adult who agreed to adopt a youth in prayer.

Our youth helped us compile a list of prayer targets for use by the entire congregation. We developed this into a bulletin insert so everyone in the congregation could take home a reminder to pray for the youth of our church."[8]

The members of Living Streams have made a commitment to build a prayer hedge around their youth. They are not going to let the Enemy draw their youth into—or keep them bound by—illicit sex, gangs, or rebellion.

Church leaders, children's ministry workers, parents—will you stand in the gap for the millennial generation—that it may be said of them as it was of King David (Acts 13:36) that he "served God's purpose in his own generation"?

TAKE IT OUT OF THE HOUSE

Try some of these prayer activities with the children in your church.

Prayer Adventure: The Prayer Room — Take children on a tour of the prayer room and explain what it's used for. Explain how each item in the room is used in prayer. Then give the children some time to pray on their own.

Prayer Adventure: The Pastor — Take the children to the pastor's study to pray for him. If he is present, the children could gather around, laying their hands on him while taking turns praying. Suggested prayers: wisdom, health and protection, time alone with God, and ability to communicate the vision to others.

Prayer Adventure: The Worship Center — Take the children on a prayer adventure to the worship center when it's vacant. Let the children lay hands on the pews or seats and pray for the person who will sit there in the upcoming weekend services.

Prayer Adventure: The Parking Lot — Take the children on a prayer adventure to the church parking lot. Ask them to pray over the cars: for the unsaved to receive God's salvation, for newcomers to feel welcome, for the families to receive understanding of God's Word.

Prayer Adventure: The Nursery — Lead children on a prayer journey to the church nursery. Let the children pray for the babies and toddlers as they touch the cribs, toys, and furniture. Suggested prayers: health and protection, to come to know the Lord at an early age, respect for authority, to receive God's love and mercy.

SATURATE YOUR CHILDREN IN PRAYER TODAY

*Dear Heavenly Father, we confess that we have under-
estimated the spiritual capacity of the children You have
entrusted to our ministry. We ask Your forgiveness for any
way that we have regarded children as less capable of hearing Your voice or praying with power than adults. Please put
Your Spirit on us so that we can have the strength, power,
ability, and creative energy to bring these little ones into Your
presence and teach them to interact with You. May we create
an atmosphere where the prayers of children are welcomed
alongside those of adults. Give our entire church a vision for
raising the bar for what our children can be and do through
prayer. Amen.*

CHAPTER 9

BECOMING A PRAYER MENTOR

> With this in mind, we constantly pray for you, that
> our God may count you worthy of his calling, and
> that by his power he may fulfill every good purpose
> of yours and every act prompted by your faith.
> (2 Thessalonians 1:11)

When George was fifteen, he and his family attended church regularly. Life was not easy, and he experienced the typical ups and
downs of teenage life. One day George came home from school to
discover his father had given up life's race. His dad had committed
suicide. George had to become the man of the house, whether he
wanted to or not, as a fifteen-year-old boy.

Years later, George and his friend Bob Biehl (author of
Mentoring: Confidence in Finding a Mentor and Becoming One) were
talking about mentoring. Bob asked George what difference it
would have made when he was fifteen if a man from the church had
said, "You know, George, there is no way on the face of the earth
that I can even begin to understand what you are feeling right now,
but I'm going to pray for you for the rest of my life, no matter where
you go or what you do. Just keep me up to date so I can know how

to pray for you. Whatever you choose to become in life, I want to be one of your life mentors, one of your lifelong friends."

By this time, the tears were dripping off George's chin. He answered, "All the difference in the world."[1]

Today mentoring is a buzzword. It doesn't mean the same thing to everyone. In his book *Mentoring*, Biehl says that mentoring begins by going to another person (usually younger or less experienced than yourself) and saying, "I'd like to be one of your life mentors, and what I mean by that is simple. I want to put you on my lifelong prayer list. Whatever you end up doing in life, I want you to know that as long as I walk the face of the earth, you have someone who is praying for you and wants to see you win. I want to help you any way I can."[2]

When I (Cheryl) was a young woman, someone did just that for me. At a time in my life when I was at a critical crossroads and spiritual crisis, a mentor made all the difference in the world! I had just moved back to Texas from Florida to be with my mom after the tragic death of my father. I was devastated, without a job, and seeking the Lord for my next step.

I was fortunate to have a praying mother, and one added benefit was that her best friend, Hazel, wanted to spend time with me — to help me develop my faith and prayer life. She never told me that was her intention and she never used the word "mentor." I certainly had no idea I was being mentored. But I suspect Hazel knew exactly what she was doing. For about seven months, Hazel and I spent some part of almost every day together. Sometimes we went out to lunch, for coffee, or for a walk in the mall. Much of the time we attended Bible studies and Christian services. Each time we were together, Hazel asked, "How are you doing? How can I pray for you? Is there anything I can do for you?"

Hazel's life marked with joy and love amazed me, yet it was her supernatural faith and mountain-moving prayers that most filled me with awe. I listened carefully to the way she phrased scriptural, positive, faith-filled prayers and determined that I would accept nothing less for my life. As I put into practice the things I was observing and absorbing, new doors began to open to me. Hazel prayed with me for God's choice of a husband and attended my wedding. She laid hands on our daughter, Nicole, as a baby and blessed her. She prayed for me and cheered me on as I spoke in my first church service and wrote my first book. My picture sits on the dresser in her bedroom, and I know she still prays for me often.

Embers of passion glow in the spirits of many young people — embers just waiting to be fanned into white-hot flames by adults like you and me. How? By mentoring young people in prayer. It's true: More is caught than taught! For three years, Jesus' disciples walked with Him, talked with Him, and prayed with Him. He showed them how to heal the sick, open the eyes of the blind, set free those who were oppressed by the Devil — and then sent them out to do the same (see Matthew 10:1; Luke 10:19; John 14:12; Acts 10:38).

When Moses turned over his leadership to Joshua, he had already been mentoring the younger man for some time. When Moses spent time in the presence of the Lord — in face-to-face conversation with Him — Joshua was close at hand to observe and learn (see Exodus 33:11). "Encourage and strengthen him," God told Moses, "for he will [cause] this people . . . to inherit the land" (Deuteronomy 3:28). Naomi taught Ruth, Elijah taught Elisha, Elizabeth taught Mary, Jesus taught the disciples, Barnabas taught Paul, Paul taught Timothy, and Priscilla and Aquila taught Apollos.

Mentoring may include evangelism, discipleship, and modeling. However, mentoring is more than any of these. The mentor is committed to seeing the protégé succeed in his or her God-given potential and is willing to commit prayers, talents, and resources to see that happen. Ideally, mentoring is a lifelong relationship, but realistically, not all of them last a lifetime. Some very productive mentoring relationships are short-term.[3] Most mentoring is informal like the relationship I had with Hazel. However, entering into formal mentoring makes the relationship intentional.

We are all definitely called to mentor our own children. But we may also be called to mentor young people who are not our children, perhaps not even in our own family. Neighbors, teachers, coaches, youth leaders, relatives, and church family—all can be praying mentors for the young people in their lives. We are to mentor, encourage, and strengthen them so that they will indeed inherit the land of God's promises!

WHY MENTORING IS SO IMPORTANT TO THE UPCOMING GENERATION

What's different about today's young people? They are more regularly exposed to negative influences than any generation before them: explicit movies and music, irreverent and immoral television shows, violent video games, Internet pornography, drugs, alcohol, rampant promiscuity, and vulgarity. At the same time, they are more regularly deprived of positive influences such as stable marriages, parents who spend time with them, and extended family close by. They are crying out for genuine, lasting connections with people.

When John was only three years old, his parents divorced. Though John's mother was loving and attentive, John lacked the love and affirmation of a father. When John was a freshman in college, he met a man who would become his spiritual father. Doug Barram, at the time a Young Life area director, had come to watch a freshman football game. John recalls that other than dyed-in-the-wool fans, *nobody* goes to freshman football games. Yet Doug was there. He stood at the sidelines at every game offering words of encouragement (blessings) to a young man who had not yet heard about Christ.

In the years that followed, Doug took a fatherly interest in John and his two brothers. Doug gave the father's blessing to three boys who very much needed it. Each brother, and even John's mother, would come to know Christ because of this man. Today John Trent is a well-known speaker, counselor, and author of more than a dozen award-winning, best-selling books, including one he coauthored with Gary Smalley, titled *The Blessing*.[4]

When Nicole was a little girl I prayed that the Lord would help Hal and me prepare her for the unique challenges of the world in which she would live. I knew that her world was going to be much different from the one in which I grew up. Little did I know that by the time Nicole was a teenager, things like school shootings, terrorism, rampant drug abuse on campus, homosexuality, and witchcraft would be commonplace.

Early on I realized quite well my own inadequacies, so I prayed that the Lord would send others to mentor Nicole in ways that I was not equipped or gifted. One rather specific prayer of mine was for God to send Nicole His highest and best teachers, both spiritually and academically. While a teacher and mentor are not the same thing, teachers can be very strong influencers in a child's life and are often the closest thing to a mentor many children ever have.

In answer to this prayer God sent into Nicole's life gracious, mature Christian women who took a special interest in her — women like Esther Ilnisky and Cindy Jacobs, who not only prayed for her and with her, but also modeled godly leadership and taught her to intercede for the nations of the world.

When Nicole reached high school, the Lord miraculously provided a partial scholarship for her to attend a private Christian school. One of her teachers was Dr. David Savidge, a true mentor of young people. When Nicole did poorly on her first few grammar tests, Dr. Savidge called to tell us he was praying for her and wanted to spend extra time helping her grasp the material. The night after Nicole made her first 100 on an exam, he brought an ice cream cake over to our house to celebrate. When Dr. Savidge saw Nicole's love and gift for photography in her work on the yearbook, he created a special photography award, which she won every year. He encouraged her to enter photography contests and invested his time to help her succeed. To our surprise, the year Nicole graduated from high school and enrolled in Southwestern College, Dr. Savidge made a switch, too. He joined the college faculty that year and he became one of Nicole's teachers once again. (You know that God will move heaven and earth, and yes, even teachers if necessary, in answer to a parent's prayers!)

THE PITS: PERSONAL INTENTIONAL TRAINING

Our family friend, a Washington pastor named Hal Perkins, decided to instill in each of his children a desire to be close to the Lord through prayer. That decision, made more than thirty years ago, has paid off. Today all of his children are involved in prayer and prayer ministry. Hal believes that *intentional* mentoring is the key to raising praying kids and notes that the family is God's best disciple-making institution. The greatest disciplers in our culture, Hal believes, are parents, entertainment, and peers. Parents must be equipped to mentor their children in overcoming the influence of media and peers.[5]

Hal's suggestions for intentional mentoring of a family are basic and foundational:

1. Pray for each family member consistently.
2. Gather your family together at least once a week as a small group to
   • *Worship*: giving praise to God for things you know about

Him and giving thanks as a family for good things, all of which are from God.

- *Word*: meditating together on God's Word and responding to what He has said to us by speaking to Him about His Word to us, praying the Word.
- *Work*: asking God for answers to two questions: "Lord, what do You want to do in our family, church, and friends?" "Lord, what do You want to do in and through us?" By consistently practicing a prayer process something like this, children are being trained to communicate with God effectively on their own and can thus learn how to lead their friends to effectively communicate with God by doing with their friends what their parents did with them.

3. Grow in your own mentoring skills by receiving small group leadership training. Your family is your "small group."

4. Establish a one-on-one "mentoring date" with each family member. Do together what you do alone in your own time with Jesus.[6]

One of Arlyn's pastors, Kurt, and his wife, Michelle, began to purposefully mentor their four daughters (then preteen and teen) in prayer in two distinct ways. Morning "quiet times" involved just the girls with Kurt. Frequently each girl would also have some one-on-one prayer time with her father. Fridays were "Lattes and TACIS" days (TACIS is the acronym for the prayer outline Thanksgiving, Adoration, Confession, Intercession, and Supplication). On these days, Kurt made lattes for everyone and they all gathered around the table for group prayer.

Family prayer times often took the form of blessings. Kurt and Michelle would put one girl in the "snuggle chair," as Kurt calls it, and everyone would take turns praying blessings over her. They would ask the Holy Spirit to show them aspects of each girl's original design and pray that God's purposes and destiny in her life be accomplished in very specific and strategic ways. When one of them was going through a difficult time, they would inquire of the Lord as to what scheme of the Enemy might be coming against her and then pray prayers of protection and spiritual warfare over her. If root heart issues were exposed, they prayed through those, as well.

Kurt admits that it has been a tremendous investment of time and effort on his and Michelle's part to make prayer such an integral part of their family life—yet it has paid great dividends spiritually in their lives, the girls' lives, and even in the lives of people around them.

As Hal's and Kurt's models illustrate, an important goal of intentionally mentoring young people in prayer is to help them learn to go into God's presence themselves, and to establish a lifestyle of effective, transformational prayer that will endure for a lifetime. It's like introducing someone to one of your good friends, knowing that they will eventually be good friends themselves and continue a life-long relationship—even if you're not around.

PRAYER MINISTRY TRAINING

Our young people have an amazing capacity for passion and zeal. They have potential far beyond what most of us dare to imagine. All they need is for someone—a parent, grandparent, youth leader, neighbor, or coach who believes in their spiritual potential—to make the investment of time to train and mentor them.

Arlyn shares how her daughter Heather has been mentored in prayer ministry:

For years Heather watched her dad and me pray with people as we ministered on prayer teams at our church. We also prayed with her at home in the same way. When needs and concerns came up, we prayed with her to identify root causes and offer prayers of repentance and engage in spiritual warfare when necessary, and to pray blessings. She saw the fruit of prayer ministry in our family's life and in the lives of others. So it was a natural move for Heather to receive training and become part of the prayer team ministry in her high school youth group, where she was also mentored by other praying adults.

One day, while ministering at a conference, Heather was on a prayer team with an adult couple ministering to a teenage boy from England. As they prayed for the boy, Heather received a strong impression from the Holy Spirit of the word "abandonment." She brought it to their attention and asked the boy what it meant to him. The boy's heart was immediately pierced—his father had left the family when he was very young and he had been sent to boarding school. Feelings of abandonment had tormented him and prevented him from receiving God's love and the love of friends and family. Heather, with her adult coaches, was able to help this young man identify the lies from the Enemy he had believed, renounce them, release his bitterness, and accept God's great love for him.

This kind of experience is powerful for teens on both the giving and receiving ends of prayer ministry. They love the relational aspect of being mentored and receiving prayer ministry—and also the highly interactive and relational aspect of being on the giving end. They see real, spiritual transformation in their own lives and in the lives of others. There's no need to convince *these* kids of the power of prayer! For a relational generation such as theirs—one that is seeking the "connection" of which many have been deprived in other areas of their lives—being mentored in personal prayer ministry is an effective way for them to experience and demonstrate the transforming love of Jesus.

MENTORING PRAYER LEADERS

Because kids are so connected to their peers, they make highly effective prayer mobilizers. When Nicole and her friend Stephanie were fifteen, they and a small group of friends started a city-wide, youth-led prayer movement in Phoenix, Arizona, called "Sacred Edge." Its purpose was to call youth to pray for the healing and restoration of their generation. Meeting the first Friday of every month, one hundred to three hundred young people came from across the city for worship and prayer.

The endeavor started small; the first night only twenty-five kids showed up, and Nicole relates that it felt like "their prayers fell to the ground." But from this humble beginning, she says, Jesus faithfully taught them how to lead, how to teach others to pray, and how to draw young people together for a powerful combination of worship and prayer.

As experienced youth prayer mobilizers, Nicole and Stephanie share some practical ideas for investing in young people to help raise them up to be prayer leaders and prayer mobilizers within the youth culture:

- **Let the youth lead.** Gather a diverse leadership team of young people, establish an adult leadership team as their covering, and release them to run with the vision. They have to own it. And believe me, they will know when they don't! When we were starting, we took a directory of churches and just started calling down the list, asking to talk to youth pastors about starting a city-wide monthly youth prayer meeting. We had not yet been told that it could not be done. So we did it.

- **Mentor young leaders.** Establish one or two adults to mentor young leaders, answer their questions, and deal with life issues as they come up. Establish regular meetings for the group to come together with their mentors and pray over the events.

- **Find "the secret place."** The group as a whole — the young leaders as well as the older — must see prayer as the first priority, and not just with lip service. It must be practiced. Prayer is the key to intimacy with Jesus and being able to discern His voice. A couple of times during the course of Sacred Edge we felt impressed by the Lord not to do any advertising for our next event. We didn't make a flyer; we made no phone calls to churches — nothing. Instead we spent our Saturday morning meeting times totally focused on prayer for our city and for the next event. And guess what? Those events were the largest of all.

- **Establish a prayer covering.** Recruit a team of adult intercessors to cover the events, the adult oversight team, and especially the young leadership team in prayer. Assign each individual an intercessor to call if he or she is struggling with something or has specific prayer needs. This is such an encouragement to them — they know that their lives are important enough to be covered in prayer.

- **Honor and encourage your young leaders.** Ask the churches represented to pay for the young leaders to go to prayer conferences to receive training and encouragement. Recognize them as prayer leaders in the city. Don't play down their calling just because they are young. This is the beginning of returning the fathers' hearts to the children and the children's hearts to the fathers (see Malachi 4:5-6; Luke 1:17).[7]

WISDOM ALONG THE WAY

When young people are on fire spiritually, a mentor is generally not needed to get them going so much as to provide wisdom along the way. That's partly because it's easy for them to get excited about their passion for Christ—and for prayer—and lose sight of the fact that wisdom and maturity are gifts from God, too!

Arlyn once chatted with the perturbed mother of a college student. Her distress stemmed from recent news that her daughter had quit her lucrative part-time job—because "Jesus said so." Now she had no income to pay her living expenses. Her parents felt somewhat taken advantage of, not to mention concerned for their daughter's well-being. They discovered that the directive had come out of a prayer time with friends who felt they were all hearing from the Lord on the girl's behalf that she was to quit her job—for no other apparent reason than "Jesus said so."

It's very possible that this girl's friends may have been hearing from the Lord when they suggested she quit her job. But by running straight from revelation to application without some wisely applied interpretation, their exuberance ended up causing a good deal of unnecessary heartache. Had they coupled what they were receiving with wisdom, sensitivity to timing issues, and the authority of her parents, they could possibly have avoided a lot of conflict. These are all things that mentors bring to the table.

Mentors also provide insight, like the time one of Arlyn's girls, Heather, came down to breakfast chuckling over an odd dream. It caught her mother's attention.

Heather related a dream that Arlyn discerned as being from the Lord. It was a poignant picture of His calling Heather to be an intercessor on behalf of the student body in her school. A light went on in her mind and she was able to see with new clarity how God wanted to use her in her junior high school. It was a spiritual "aha" moment on which Arlyn was able to capitalize by offering some timely wisdom, guidance, and insight.

Identifying and seizing those teachable moments is key to mentoring young people in prayer. Sitting down for formalized prayer times with them becomes less and less frequent as they develop lives and schedules of their own and move toward adulthood. Many times the guidance process takes the form of "debriefing" after the teen has had prayer encounters elsewhere — either personally or with others — and needs to unpack the experience with wisdom.

This requires great sensitivity, patience, and grace on behalf of the mentor. If the challenge for young people is to accept the accountability of an older person's correction and guidance with humility and submissiveness, then the challenge for older folks is to offer guidance and correction without quenching their fire. Young people can be idealistic and uninhibited by past failures. In their minds, anything is possible. They bring great faith to the table in prayer.

May we never be the "old wineskins" that Jesus spoke of in Luke 5! God is doing a powerful thing in our young people, and the prayer lives of the children in your life may look different from yours. That's okay. Be willing to let God be God and move in their lives in unique and powerful ways. You may learn a thing or two from them, instead of the other way around! Be prepared for the wisdom encountered along the way as you mentor youth in prayer to be a two-way street.

TAKE IT OUT OF THE HOUSE

When we pray *for* the young people God has called us to walk beside, we provide a canopy or covering that protects them and paves the way for God to work in their lives. Some people like to call this a prayer shield, which is a great image.

As a practical prayer exercise, put the name of the young

person (or people) whom you are mentoring into the Scriptures below and pray these passages aloud to the Lord. There are enough passages listed to help build a substantial prayer shield over the young people in your life:

Salvation, identity, and security in Christ—Galatians 2:20; 2 Corinthians 5:17

Finding and fulfilling their God-given purpose—Jeremiah 29:11; Psalm 139:13-16

Godly character and morals—Psalm 24:4; James 1:27; Romans 12:2

Protection from evil—Psalm 34:7; Job 1:10; Psalm 84:11

Grounding in the Word—Psalm 1:2; 119:11; John 14:26; 17:17

An intimate, Spirit-filled relationship with God—Ephesians 5:18; Isaiah 30:20-21

Strength to resist temptations—1 Corinthians 10:13; James 1:14-15

Submission to authority—Hebrews 13:17; 1 Peter 5:5; Ephesians 6:2-3

Endurance and commitment—2 Timothy 2:3; 2 Thessalonians 3:13

Wisdom in relationships—Psalm 1:1; James 1:19

Wisdom in handling finances—Genesis 22:14; Psalm 37:25; Philippians 4:19

Powerful witness—Acts 1:8; 4:29-31; 1 Peter 3:15

Passion for the lost and for the nations—Isaiah 61:4; Luke 4:18-19

SATURATE YOUR CHILD WITH PRAYER TODAY

Dear Lord, I want to be one who raises up and releases a new generation of prayer warriors. Show me those You have put in my path who have a calling to change the course of history through prayer. Help me to sow into them the secrets of prayer You have taught me. In the middle of a busy life, show me how to seize special moments with those who would benefit from spending time with me. Strengthen my prayer life, because I know I cannot give to others what I do not have myself. Give me a Spirit-filled prayer life—one that will serve as a model to the youth whose lives I touch. Amen.

CHAPTER 10

REVIVAL KIDS . . . TURN 'EM LOOSE!

From the lips of children and infants
  you have ordained praise
because of your enemies,
  to silence the foe and the avenger. (Psalm 8:2)

"Have you heard what's happened to the children?" The tone of the woman's voice sounded urgent.

"No, what?" I responded anxiously.

"You'd better come downstairs to the basement and see for yourself," she said.

I (Cheryl) grabbed my husband's hand and we hurriedly made our way through the crowd to the stairwell that led to the bottom floor of the World Torch Center. It was May 17, 1995, the first day of GCOWE (Global Consultation on World Evangelism) in Seoul, South Korea. Hal and I felt privileged to be delegates to this history-making conference. We were even more excited that Nicole, just thirteen at the time, had been among forty kids from around the world selected to participate in the children's prayer track. Their mission? To pray for the salvation of the children of the world.

But now I wasn't so sure about our decision. Perhaps it had

not been such a good idea to bring her to a foreign country, to be transported by bus drivers we didn't know to venues that seemed to change every time we were issued a new schedule. As we rounded the corner to the basement opening, my anxiety mounted. *What had happened to the children?* As we entered the room I could not believe my eyes. There, lying prostrate in a large circle, were forty praying children — their arms wrapped around each other as they wept over the lost souls of the children of the world.

Leading this special group of children was Esther Ilnisky, a pastor's wife who knew how to release children in prayer and intercession. Because of the short attention span of this age group (ages five to fifteen), Esther had brought plenty of games and activities to keep the children occupied when they were not praying. She planned a number of prayer sessions throughout the day, each one scheduled to last about fifteen minutes.

However, the first prayer session had not gone as expected. The children did not stop praying after fifteen minutes, and they did not stop praying after fifty minutes. In fact, the praying and weeping continued for *four hours and twenty minutes!*

When the prayer time was over, I knelt down beside a little boy who looked to be about five years old. "How did you manage to pray for four hours and twenty minutes?" I asked.

"Oh, we didn't know we prayed so long," he said. "We thought we'd been praying only about twenty minutes."

From the history of revivals, I was reminded that whenever children begin to pray, revival is hastened.

AS THE DAYS CONTINUED . . .

Without any prompting from Esther, the lengthy prayer sessions of the children continued each day throughout the conference. On the third day, three children on different sides of the room saw a vision of the children in Zaire (now Congo), Africa, where Ebola Fever had just broken out. This deadly disease—which has no cure—causes its victims to die a painful death in a matter of days. All three children described to their leaders the same scene without any variation.

"We must pray for the children of Zaire!" they exclaimed. "God, stop the Ebola virus," they pleaded. "Stop the Ebola virus!" This was no superficial prayer meeting. The children beseeched their heavenly Father on behalf of the souls of the children of Zaire. They commanded the Devil, in Jesus' name, to take his hands off these precious African children. And they would not let go of God until His power was released to strike His final blow upon the deadly Ebola virus.

Seven days later, the day after the conference ended, the World Health Organization declared on front-page headlines of newspapers around the world, "Ebola is coming under control."[1]

The *New York Times* reported on May 27, 1995: "With only six new cases of Ebola infection reported in Zaire over the last week [since the day the children prayed] the World Health Organization said today that the epidemic of the deadly viral disease in the African country was 'coming under control.'" The article went on to say that those six new cases had been attributed to the incubation period—which meant not a single person had been infected since the day the children prayed![2]

Youth and children like these are key players in accomplishing God's purposes on earth. Many Christian leaders today believe that we are on the verge of the greatest revival in the history of our nation. And children and teenagers are absolutely essential to the breakthrough we're looking for.

For example, Arlyn's church saw eighty to ninety junior high and high school students receive Christ in a four-month period, due to the fervent prayers and concerted outreach of its youth group of only about fifty kids. On the first outreach night, Arlyn was amazed to see about fifty teens stream into the prayer rooms to receive Christ. She was even more amazed to see that the prayer teams who led them to Christ, prayed with them to break bondages of the Enemy in their lives, and prayed powerful blessings over them were mostly other teenagers!

Emboldened by their success (probably in much the same way the disciples were in Luke 10 when they returned from their first official "outreach" trip), the kids began praying for even more students to come to Christ. But a couple of months later, as time for a second outreach event came along, the kids came under spiritual attack. Seeds of resentment, misunderstanding, and disunity sprouted in their midst. Their relationships became tainted by arguments, factions, and backbiting. Would the ground they had taken be so easily lost?

The day of the outreach event, without any adult intervention, the kids' spiritual eyes were opened. They realized that what they were experiencing was not natural, but spiritual. By phone, e-mail, and text message, eight of the students quickly arranged a meeting, gathering that afternoon at the church where they determined they would not let the Enemy rob them of their unity nor of the souls of their friends for whom they'd been interceding. They confessed their sin to each another, repented before the Lord together, and blessed one another.

That night, thirty-five more teenagers received Christ. During the following months, the youth group swelled with new believers. There were so many baptisms they had to spread them out over several weeks.

KIDS' ROLE IN REVIVAL HISTORY

These stories are reminiscent of what we discover in the histories of revivals: the deep faith and profound influence of praying children. They have often played a significant role in revival — many times leading the way.

In the early 1720's a sixteen-year-old named Nikolaus Zinzendorf formed a prayer group with five other teenagers at his school in Germany. They were called the "Order of the Grain of Mustard Seed." This name was most appropriate—the group became a seedbed of revival that spread throughout Germany and even beyond.[3]

In America, student-led prayer groups in 1806 and 1886 were responsible for starting major revival movements that resulted in a great expansion of world missions. One such revival movement, called the Student Volunteer Movement, was a fulfillment of a vision that sent nearly twenty thousand praying young people into missionary service over a thirty-year period.[4]

And let's not forget the sixteen-year-old girl in Andrew Murray's church in Wellington, South Africa, who led a revival prayer movement among her peers in 1860. Murray was at first threatened by this girl and her student prayer movement; it is reported that he later repented of his opposition. Murray went on to write more than 120 books, the last of which was a call to pastors worldwide to unite in prayer for revival as the only hope for their generation.[5] One young girl helped change the course of history in the body of Christ worldwide.

THE ACCELERATING YOUTH
PRAYER MOVEMENT

In recent years we've watched the acceleration of the children's and youth prayer movement worldwide, seeing and hearing some amazing reports. Many nations around the world are experiencing outpourings of prayer among their children.

In London, Pete Greig, author of *Red Moon Rising*, is leading a 24/7 youth prayer movement that has exploded to more than fifty countries since its inception in 1999. An army of radical young people is now praying simultaneously night and day around the world.

Eleven years after the conference in Seoul, where there was such a dramatic move of God among the children, some of the same leaders gathered at another conference that convened in southeast Asia in 2006. Laying a foundation for the future, 170 men, women, and children—representing at least thirty-five nations—met to pray, network, and plan toward the development of a global prayer network for kids.

In India, one ministry redeems outcast street children and trains them to be intercessors, evangelists, worship leaders, and church planters. They are the lowest of the caste system; some are considered "untouchables." Many are orphans due to poverty, leprosy, and AIDS. Some are tribal, some gypsies, and some prostitutes.

In 1987, God spoke to a young man about raising up these "throwaway children" as an army of intercessors to "reach the lost, heal the sick, and prophesy to the nations." Not only has he been doing it, he has been actively training others to reach the lost, too. The Indian government has taken notice and subsidizes the children's care—and continues to send them even more children to redeem and raise up as prayer warriors.

In another Asian country are six children's prayer towers where children meet three times a week to pray for their communities. More than a thousand children from around the nation gather to pray several times a year, such as during the Global Day of Prayer and the World Wide Day of Prayer for Children at Risk. And in eighty-five cities throughout Indonesia, there are more than 170 leaders and sixty thousand children involved in prayer ministry. These young prayer warriors are praying for the transformation of their communities and nation. Their leaders are currently developing curriculum to replicate what they are doing in every city in Indonesia.

A seventeen-year-old girl named Eunice began a ministry to connect youth from all over her country in prayer for their nation and to join kids from all around the globe to exchange news reports of what God is doing in various countries. This vision, birthed out of Ezekiel 37:10, has encouraged young people to redeem the Internet for the Lord by way of a 24/7 Web-based prayer community.[6]

WHAT ABOUT AMERICA?

In the U.S. and Canada, nearly three million students are gathering at their school flagpoles each September for See You at the Pole, where they are praying for their teachers, classmates, and revival on their campuses. Growing numbers of youth are combining prayer with fasting, sometimes for prolonged periods of time.[7]

Perhaps one of the greatest signs of a coming revival in our time was the gathering of some 400,000 youth (many with their parents) at the mall in Washington, D.C., on Labor Day weekend 2000 for twelve hours of prayer and fasting for the nation. Hal and I attended this powerful gathering with Nicole, who had spent that year working as youth facilitator for The Call DC. As far as the eye could see, interceding teenagers were standing, sitting, kneeling, and lying prostrate on the ground as they cried out, "We're here to start a Jesus Revolution! Enough is enough! God, turn our nation back to You!"

Pray! magazine devoted an entire issue to the topic of praying teenagers. One article reported that high school students in Modesto, California, are doing Jericho-style prayerwalks around every school in the city. In Littleton, Colorado, students are on their way to establishing a prayer group on every school campus in their community. Young people from Portland, Oregon, to Buffalo, New York, are involved in intensive prayer efforts.

"What's going on?" the author of the article asked.

There seems to be an unprecedented, unplanned, unusual, and unstoppable explosion of prayer among youth! It's unprecedented, at least in modern times, because of the sheer number of participants. It's unplanned because it's not the result of some new youth ministry program or activity. It appears to be a quite spontaneous work of the Holy Spirit, and nobody is trying to control it (good luck if you attempt to do so!). It's unusual because such passion for prayer is not what's expected from a postmodern, relativistic, diversity-embracing culture. And it's unstoppable because it can't be legislated out of the schools—you can take prayer out of schools, but you can't take praying students out![8]

This story about a young girl named Elizabeth Cartwright and her vision and determination illustrates just how true that statement is.

In 1962, the U.S. Supreme Court voted to remove prayer from American classrooms. I knew that as a fact of history, but in my small town in Texas, it wasn't a fact of life. In my hometown, everybody knew everybody and most people were raised in church. We continued to pray at football games and other public events, and it was never a problem. At least not until my junior year, when the school board decided to enforce the law. They passed an ordinance prohibiting the prayer that was spoken over the loudspeaker before every football game.

Once that happened, people also began to question the legality of the campus ministry that met every morning for prayer and once a week during lunch. Like many in the student body, I was shocked at the changes. As president of the campus ministry, I found myself in the middle of the biggest spiritual battle I'd ever encountered.

I went to the superintendent, who was also a Christian. "Why is this happening? What can we do about it?"

"I'm sorry. There's nothing I can do," he said. "If anything changes, it will have to be you students who take action."

But we're just a bunch of teens! I thought. What can we possibly do?

Since no one in an authority position in our school would help, I decided to go over their heads—straight to God. I prayed fervently for His wisdom. He asked me what biblical example I could follow. I took a hard look at what people in the Bible did when they were forbidden by law to worship God, and I discovered something amazing—they worshiped anyway!

I gathered a group of students, and we began to pray that God would help us fight just like those in the Bible had done. Still, we were clueless about what to do. One student's father presented a plan to the school board that would provide a way for us to pray, and it had huge support in the community.

But the school board rejected it.

Then God gave us an idea that was risky, but we weren't about to give up. At the next football game, as fans filled the stadium, we all took our places. Since the law had been enforced, instead of prayer, the stadium now had a moment of silence before the football game.

But instead of obeying the silent rule, our group began saying the Lord's Prayer out loud. Then the most unexpected thing happened. The student body joined. Parents joined. Children joined. Teachers and faculty joined. The prayer spread like fire across the stadium. Even the fans on the opposing team joined in our act of rebellion!

The moment we said "Amen," the stadium exploded into applause and cheering.

*And later the school board approved a plan allowing us to
pray. At games after that amazing night, a standing ovation
followed the opening prayer."*[9]

TAKING IT TO THE STREETS

One year in Phoenix, the week before school started, students
took vans filled with praying teenagers to intercede at forty high
schools. They beseeched God for His revival fire to hit the high
school campuses that fall. Later, students reported that God was
showing up in extraordinary ways with public repentance of sin
and many miraculous salvations.

One morning before school one of these students, Christina,
felt an urgency to drive to an abortion clinic to pray for God to
expose Satan's works of darkness there. Within hours the media
caught wind of an incident that had occurred in the clinic. Only
two weeks later the clinic was closed.

Arlyn and I know of a church youth group who had a heart
for evangelism and to see their campuses come to Christ. Several
kids who went to the same high school organized a weekly prayer
meeting on campus with some other Christian kids. As they
prayed together regularly for the salvation of their classmates, the
Lord birthed in their hearts an idea for an "outreach." They bought
cases of soda and brought them out at lunchtime in the cafeteria,
announcing loudly, "Free soda! Free soda!"

When a large crowd had gathered for the free soda, three of
the kids — one by one — jumped up on a lunch table and began to
give their testimonies of how Jesus Christ had changed their lives.
When they gave an invitation, seventeen students received Christ
that day. A few months later, they did the same thing, the same
way. This time, more than thirty students received Christ!

The youth pastors and youth leaders of these kids were not

allowed on campus. Yet because they were effectively discipled and mentored in prayer and passion for Jesus, these students were well-equipped to pray and lead their classmates to Christ all by themselves!

One of the most incredible examples of children being used in intercessory prayer for the unsaved was during the well-known revival at Brownsville Assembly of God in Pensacola, Florida. One entire event was captured on video. Vann Lane, their children's pastor at the time, narrates the video, explaining to viewers what they are hearing in the background — the sound of children in deep travail.

Because of the ongoing revival, most of the church members were involved every night as workers. Thousands of people were coming daily from all over the world to be touched by the revival, and every adult was needed. But their children still had homework, still needed rest from the late nights, and so on. So Pastor Vann let them stay with him in the children's room during the services. The room contained a big screen with a live feed from the main auditorium so the children could see what was happening in the adult service.

One night as the children were playing, Pastor Vann noticed that one at a time, the children stopped what they were doing and began watching the live feed. Soon, they all spontaneously began to go into prayer. That prayer turned into the most intense, agonizing travail as the children began to wail in intercession with abandonment.

Stunned at what God was doing through the children, Pastor Vann guided them down the hall into an area hidden from the view of the audience. It was right next to the platform where evangelist Steve Hill was feverishly preaching to the lost. Ushers brought cordless mics to where the children were, and the chilling sound of their voices was piped into the main auditorium so the adults could hear what they were doing. Periodically you can hear one child screaming out, "No! No! No!" with hair-raising intensity. It seemed they were crying out against abuses of others as though they were those people. Once you hear these voices you can never be the same again.[10] The children prayed like this for almost an hour and during that time several hundred unbelieving and backslidden adults jumped out of their seats and ran to the altar to surrender their lives to Jesus Christ.[11]

THE IMPACT OF PRAYING KIDS

It is important that we encourage this passion for prayer when we see it, not quench it—so the fires of revival can be birthed again from their prayers. Our youth have the potential to make a huge difference in their world and ours through their prayer lives and their ministry for Christ. They are the future leaders of the Christian world movement, and adults know it. Older Christians are often inspired to follow young people as they begin to manifest a passion and proactiveness toward the things of God.

I believe that during the dawn of the twenty-first century God is up to something more expansive than we have previously imagined. From my vantage point, the children and youth take center stage!

One day as I was going about my housework, I heard an urgent shout from my daughter. "Come quick, Mom!" Nicole called, as she leaned over the balcony of our two-story home, gazing at the living room below. "I just saw a vision of our house totally filled with praying teenagers!"

I don't know how it all came about, but within a few weeks, our home had become the rally point for regular youth prayer meetings. Every Monday night and all day every Saturday, twenty to thirty praying kids packed into our home. They were every-where—lying prostrate on the living room floor, praying in groups in the kitchen, curled up on the furniture and in the corners of the family room, sitting and standing along the stairwell.

"A new breed of children—righteous seed—who are destined to fulfill God's eternal plans and purposes, is emerging on the world scene for the new millennium!" says Esther Ilnisky. "They are being birthed and entrusted to God-fearing parents to be nurtured and equipped for this hour. Empowered by the Holy Spirit, they will rise up as a mighty prayer force to petition God on behalf of their generation and, in the mighty name of Jesus, conquer Satan's demonic forces." [12]

As Isaiah says, "A little child will lead them" (11:6).

THE BATTLE FOR THE RIGHTEOUS SEED

The outpouring of the Holy Spirit on our own children will not come through token prayers but by wrestling in fasting and prayer against sin, apathy, and self-indulgence. Our culture has taught America's children to feast and play. The times demand they *fast* and *pray*.

Today's children and teens are under constant assault from many sources, including satanic attack. They are extremely vulnerable to all kinds of evil influences at one of the most difficult times of their lives—physically and emotionally. While many adults are writing them off as irrational, uncontrollable, moody, and unpredictable, God desires to do a powerful work in the lives of our youth.

Satan's intent, on the other hand, since the beginning of time, has been to devour the righteous seed: "The dragon stood in front of the woman who was about to give birth, so that he might devour her child the moment it was born" (Revelation 12:4). Satan sought to destroy Joseph, Moses, and Jesus, and he seeks to destroy our precious youth today! This has become increasingly evident with the rash of tragic school shootings in our nation, not to mention the toll of abortion and inner-city violence. Countless more are lost to destructive lifestyles and deceptive worldly philosophies.

We as parents and as the church will be remiss if we do not affirm their calling and do battle for them in prayer. It is important that we not only train our children and youth to be mighty prayer warriors, but also come alongside them to do battle in the heavenlies on their behalf.

As we do, "there will be waves of intercessors and young prayer warriors taking their rightful place within leadership of the global movement of prayer, with the blessing, encouragement and mentorship of the older generations who understand the importance of unleashing them to fulfill the destiny to which God is calling them."[13]

Who will pass on the power of prayer to the next generation?

Who will intercede for them?

Who will teach them to hear God's voice and train them for spiritual battle?

We will—and then we'll turn 'em loose!

DISCUSSION QUESTIONS

CHAPTER 1:
A CHILD'S ORIGINAL DESIGN

1. Can you identify some of the ways that God has uniquely designed your child or the children in your life? Which have you observed through natural means? Which have been revealed to you through prayer?
2. Discuss how your child's original design may affect his or her prayer style. What modes of communication might be most comfortable for him or her when relating to God?
3. How might praying to see God's original design for a child be a benefit in a classroom or Sunday school-type setting? Discuss ways to apply this concept with children other than your own and in secular as well as home or ministry settings.

CHAPTER 2:
MAKING YOUR HOME A HOUSE OF PRAYER

1. Referring to chapter 2, take note of anything that inspired you, provoked new thoughts, or challenged you in some way. Share those thoughts with the group, along with ways you plan to incorporate those prayer concepts into your own home.
2. Discuss the strategic roles of both moms and dads in praying with and for their children. How are they often the same?

How might they differ? What do you sense God saying to you, personally, as you consider these truths about parents and prayer?

3. Is prayer in your household a first response—or a last resort? Come up with a list of ideas for making prayer a priority for your family. What are some ways you can include your children in praying about your family's needs and concerns? What are some ways you can make your home a "prayer rest stop" for others?

CHAPTER 3:
THE POWER OF BLESSING

1. What did you learn from this chapter about the power of praying blessings? Review the three elements of the parental blessing. What are some of the benefits of giving a parental blessing to your children, and what might be some of the consequences of withholding them?

2. Was your family of origin marked more by expressing spoken blessings or withholding them? How has this influenced your ability to bless your own children or any other children in your life?

3. What are some practical ways that you can begin cultivating the practice of praying blessings in your home? How can you take these into your community, workplace, or ministry? Share these with the group and make a note of them for follow-up.

CHAPTER 4:
HEALING PRAYERS FOR HURTING FAMILIES

1. Discuss the idea of the "transactional nature of prayer" (see pages 65-66). Is this concept new to you? How does it give you fresh hope for the power and effectiveness of prayer to access the resources of heaven in a way that accomplishes healing in human hearts, lives, children, marriages, and families?

2. What are some specific situations in your family that could benefit from healing prayer?

3. Divide your group into smaller groups of two to four persons each. Spend some time in listening prayer together. With the idea of "grown-ups going first," ask the Holy Spirit to reveal to each person any personal "strongholds" or areas of unresolved bitterness in his own heart that may be resulting in wrong or hurtful attitudes and actions in his life and family. Encourage each person to offer prayers of confession and repentance, specifically granting forgiveness where forgiveness is needed. Then, as a group, pray for one another (and each other's children) that these "roots and their fruits" would be healed by the power, love, and truth of Jesus Christ.

CHAPTER 5:
CLOSING DOORS TO THE ENEMY

1. Read Ephesians 6:10-12. Note that prayer is listed as part of the armor and weaponry of the Christian (see verse 18). Also read 2 Corinthians 10:3-5. Based on these Scriptures and what you read in chapter 5, describe how prayer can be a "divinely powerful weapon" in the battle against evil that our children face in this world.

2. Is the practice of looking at people, things, and situations through spiritual eyes instead of physical eyes a new or challenging one for you? Why or why not?

3. Did the Lord bring any objects to your mind that you need to remove from your home?

4. Can you identify any generational sins in your family that are affecting (or have the potential to affect) your children? Share them with the group and take time to pray with one another. Remember the four Rs as you do: repent, rebuke, replace, and receive (see pages 89-91).

5. What are some ways that Christian parents and ministry

leaders can be "gatekeepers" in their homes and ministries — those who will be on the alert to identify and shut,
through prayer, any open doors to the Enemy in the lives of
those whom God has entrusted to their spiritual care?

CHAPTER 6:
PRAYER TRAINING 101

1. What are some ways you can help your children develop a
   personal relationship with God through prayer? Have they
   already received Christ as Savior? If not, might they be ready
   to pray that prayer with you?
2. Take note of the seven key components of teaching children
   to pray. Which ones are already established in your child's
   prayer life? Which ones are you challenged to implement in a
   new or more emphasized way, and how might you do this?
3. If you are involved in children's ministry, which of the seven
   elements are already a part of your current curriculum or ministry philosophy and practice? Which ones would you like to
   develop?
4. Do you have the expectation that hearing distinctively from
   the Holy Spirit can and should be a part of prayer? What
   are some ways that you, personally, hear God's voice? How
   have you communicated and modeled these for your children?
   What are some ways that you would like to do so?
5. How can learning to pray God's Word be a benefit to children? Can you think of some specific Scripture passages that
   you think would be good to turn into prayers with and for the
   children in your life? Make a list and begin praying them on a
   regular basis.

CHAPTER 7:
FURTHER UP AND FURTHER IN

1. How can a child's desire for adventure and action be satisfied by prayer? Does this fit in with your expectation and experience of what prayer is like? Why or why not?

2. What did you learn about the concept of the prayer closet? How can you use this concept to teach your child more about prayer?

3. Consider the ways that prayer may sometimes result in supernatural experiences, such as those the early church experienced in Acts 4:31, Peter's and Cornelius's experiences in Acts 10, and that of Paul and Silas in the Philippian jail (see Acts 16:25-26). Take turns sharing some of the supernatural results of prayer that you and the people in your group have experienced. How have these experiences helped you, your family, or your ministry fulfill Psalm 78:4, NLT: "We will not hide these truths from our children; we will tell the next generation about the glorious deeds of the LORD, about his power and his mighty wonders"?

4. Note this chapter's suggestions for "adventures" in prayer, such as fasting, prayerwalking, spiritual authority, and warfare. How do they challenge your child's (or your children's ministry's) current prayer values and lifestyle? Which are you inspired to implement? What are some ways you might do that? Share these with the group.

CHAPTER 8:
THE ROLE OF THE CHURCH

1. Chapter 8 talks about the need to abandon "old wineskins" of children's ministry—the old wineskins being "our own limited notions of what children are or aren't capable of spiritually" (see page 124)—in favor of new wineskins or new

expectations. How have your expectations of children and prayer already been raised as you have been reading *Prayer-Saturated Kids*?

2. Is prayer an obvious priority in your church or children's ministry? With your ministry team, pray and ask God to show you ways that your ministry can be a "house of prayer for children." Spend a few minutes in listening prayer. Then ask each team member to share what he or she senses the Holy Spirit speaking about raising the value and visibility of prayer in your ministry.

3. If you are a pastor or children's ministry leader, what are some practical ways that you can take a greater role in imparting spiritual life to your church's children's ministry in the area of prayer?

4. If you are a parent with a child in a Sunday school (or other children's ministry) program, what are some practical ways you can encourage and help your child's ministry leaders make prayer a more dynamic part of the ministry? What might this look like in a practical way?

CHAPTER 9:
BECOMING A PRAYER MENTOR

1. Were you ever mentored as a young person? If so, how did that experience shape you? If not, how might it have made a difference in your life? As you share these thoughts with the group, brainstorm together about ways that each of you can apply what you have learned—both from experience and from this chapter—to the relationships you currently have with young people.

2. Reread the models that pastors Hal and Kurt used as they mentored their own children in prayer (see pages 144-146). How do their examples inspire you in your own parenting?

3. If your children are older and you have not mentored them

in prayer up to this point, what are some practical, relational ways that you can begin to incorporate prayer mentoring into your relationship with them? Think in terms of mentoring your children not only in their personal prayer life but also in preparing them to serve in prayer ministry leadership.

4. If you are a pastor or youth leader, how might you begin to cast a vision for—and incorporate—prayer mentoring into your youth ministry? Again, think of mentoring youth in their personal prayer lives as well as equipping them for prayer ministry leadership.

CHAPTER 10:
REVIVAL KIDS . . . TURN 'EM LOOSE!

1. Which stories about "revival kids" from past or contemporary church history were the most inspiring to you? Talk about the potential you see in your own children—or the children in your life—to have this kind of impact on the world around them through their prayers.

2. What are ways that adults can help create environments in which kids can be "let loose" in revival-type praying? How might the adults need to be *more* involved? How might they need to be *less* involved? Discuss how and why adults may need to be hands-off versus hands-on and how to discern when each stance is necessary.

3. Plan an intercessory prayer meeting on behalf of the children represented by your group. Have a time of intercession and spiritual battle. Pray *for* God's designs and purposes to be accomplished in and through their lives. Pray *against* the schemes of the Enemy that seek to thwart and corrupt God's plans. Intercede for your children—that they truly will be prayer-saturated revival kids!

RESOURCES

Fischer, Becky. *Redefining Children's Ministry in the 21st Century* (Bismarck, ND: Kids in Ministry International, 2005).

Fuller, Cheri. *When Mothers Pray* (Sisters, OR: Multnomah, 2001).

Fuller, Cheri. *When Teens Pray*, with Ron Luce (Sisters, OR: Multnomah, 2002).

Cheri Fuller's ministry website, *FamiliesPrayUSA* (http://www. cherifuller.com).

Harvest Prayer Ministries (http://www.harvestprayer.com). Click on "Family Prayer" for links to various children's prayer ministries and resources.

Ilnisky, Esther. *Let the Children Pray* (Ventura, CA: Regal, 2000).

Jacobs, Cindy. *Deliver Us from Evil* (Ventura, CA: Regal, 2001).

Moms in Touch International (http://www.momsintouch.org).

Perkins, Hal. *If Jesus Were a Parent.* (USA, 2006).

*Pray*Kids! (http://www.praykids.com).

PrayKids! Teacher's Guide: A Hands-On Guide for Developing Kids Who Pray (Colorado Springs, CO: *Pray!* Books/NavPress, 2005).

Smalley, Gary and John Trent. *The Blessing* (Nashville: Nelson, 2004).

Swope, Mary Ruth. *Bless Your Child Every Day* (Phoenix: Swope Enterprises, 1992).

Wilson, Randy and Lisa. *Daddy's Blessing* (Colorado Springs, CO: Faith Parenting, 2001).

NOTES

CHAPTER 1

1. Charles F. Boyd, *Different Children, Different Needs* (Sisters, OR: Multnomah, 2005), 18.
2. Dutch Sheets, *Authority in Prayer* (Bloomington, MN: Bethany, 2006), 28–29.
3. Cynthia Bezek, "Wired for Prayer: Do You Know Your Child's Calling?" *PrayKids!* 21 (2004): 8.
4. Cheri Fuller, *When Children Pray* (Sisters, OR: Multnomah, 1998), 123.
5. Gary Smalley and John Trent, *The Blessing* (Nashville: Nelson, 2004), 109.
6. Smalley and Trent, 134.

CHAPTER 2

1. Kim Butts, *The Praying Family* (Chicago: Moody, 2003), 112.
2. Gallup Poll, 1993.
3. James Strong, *Strong's New Exhaustive Concordance of the Bible* (Nashville: Nelson, 1995), s.vv. "tsaphah," "shamar."
4. Edward W. Goodrick and John R. Kohlenberger III, *The NIV Exhaustive Concordance* (Grand Rapids, MI: Zondervan, 1990), 1598, 1643.
5. Quin Sherrer and Ruthanne Garlock, *How to Pray for Your Family and Friends* (Ann Arbor, MI: Servant, 1990), 67–68.
6. Excerpted from Josh McDowell, *Youth Ministry Handbook*

(Nashville: Word, 2000), 11–13.

7. Butts, 25–26.

8. Bobbie Wolgemuth, "The Prayer Project," *Focus on the Family*, February 1997, 6–7.

9. Dutch Sheets, *The Beginner's Guide to Intercession* (Ventura, CA: Regal, 2001), 159–160.

10. Edward K. Rowell, *Fresh Illustrations for Preaching and Teaching* (Grand Rapids, MI: Baker, 1997), 165.

CHAPTER 3

1. Derek Packard, *Daddy's Blessing*, VHS (Colorado Springs, CO: CV Studios, 2002).

2. Sally Meredith, "The Power of Blessing," in *Heritage Builders* (Colorado Springs, CO: Focus on the Family, 2003), 17.

3. Mary Ruth Swope, *Bless Your Child Every Day* (Phoenix: Swope Enterprises, 1992), 1–4.

4. Bill Gothard, *The Power of Spoken Blessings* (Sisters, OR: Multnomah, 2004), 31.

5. Gothard, 13–14.

6. Gary Smalley and John Trent, *The Blessing* (Nashville: Nelson, 2004), 67.

7. Packard, *Amen Simulcast.*

CHAPTER 4

1. Stormie O'Martian, *Lord, I Want to Be Whole* (Nashville: Nelson, 2000), 92.

2. Cheri Fuller, *When Families Pray* (Sisters, OR: Multnomah, 1999), 31–32.

CHAPTER 5

1. Chuck D. Pierce and Rebecca Wagner Sytsema, *Protecting Your Home from Spiritual Darkness* (Ventura, CA: Regal, 2004), 47–49.

2. Mike and Cindy Riches, *Concept of the 4 R's*, developed by Destiny City Church, Tacoma, WA.

CHAPTER 6

1. Keith Wooden, *Teaching Children to Pray* (Grand Rapids, MI: Zondervan, 1992), 27.
2. Alvin J. Vander Griend, *The Praying Church Sourcebook* (Grand Rapids, MI: Church Development Resources, 1990), 59.
3. Susan Lingo, *Teaching Our Children to Pray* (Cincinnati: Standard, 1997), 73.
4. Dick Eastman, "Hotline from Heaven," *PrayKids!* 6 (2001): 1.
5. Jocelyn Shover, "My Sister Bethany," *PrayKids!* 6 (2001): 3.
6. Jonathan Graf, *Nuts and Bolts of Developing Children in Prayer* (audiotape of lecture at NALCPL, Colorado Springs, CO, 2001).
7. Mike and Dottie Steczo, "Children's Prayer Styles," *Pray!*, May/June 2001, 11.

CHAPTER 7

1. Adapted from C. S. Lewis, *The Last Battle* (New York: Macmillan, 1956), 147–158.
2. Concept of the meaning and mystery of the prayer closet developed by Sandi Powelson.
3. Arlyn Lawrence, *PrayKids! Teacher's Guide* (Colorado Springs, CO: NavPress, 2005), 149.
4. Steve Hawthorne, "Stepping Out with Jesus," *PrayKids!* (2005): 8.
5. Lawrence, 41.
6. Allyson Miller, "Enemy, Get Lost," *PrayKids!* (2005): 3.
7. From "The Inexplicable Prayers of Ruby Bridges" by Robert Coles, *Finding God at Harvard*, Kelly Monroe, ed. (Grand Rapids, MI: Zondervan: 1996), 33-34.
8. *Webster's New 20th Century Dictionary of the English*

Language, ed. Jean L. McKechnie (William Collins and World Publishing Co., 1977), s.v. "curse."

9. Adapted from Mike Riches, *Strongholds: Understanding and Destroying Satan's Schemes* (Tacoma, WA: Revalesio Ministries, 2005), 120–123.

CHAPTER 8

1. Eric Reed, "Let the Children Pray," *Today's Christian,* May/June 2002, 14.
2. Bubba Stahl, interview by Cheryl Sacks, February 2001, Bourne, TX.
3. Sue Curran, *The Praying Church* (Blountville, TN: Shekinah Publishing, 1987), 85–86.
4. Becky Fischer, *Redefining Children's Ministry in the 21st Century* (Bismarck, ND: Kids in Ministry International, 2005), 160–165.
5. For more ideas like this, see *PrayKids! Teacher's Guide: A Hands-On Guide for Developing Kids Who Pray* (Colorado Springs, CO: NavPress, 2005).
6. George Barna, *Transforming Children into Spiritual Champions* (Ventura, CA: Issachar Resources, 2003), 111.
7. See http://www.praykids.com.
8. Kurt Cotter, interview by Cheryl Sacks, August 1997.

CHAPTER 9

1. Bob Biehl, *Mentoring* (Nashville: Broadman, Holman, 1996), 6.
2. Biehl, 5.
3. Biehl, 19–20.
4. Gary Smalley and John Trent, *The Blessing* (Nashville: Nelson, 2004), 203.
5. Hal Perkins, "Family Houses of Prayer Everywhere," *Empowered,* no. 2 (Summer 2002), 12.

6. Perkins, 12-13.
7. Nicole Sacks and Stephanie Seekins, "Starting a City-wide, Youth-led Prayer Movement," *Empowered*, no. 2 (Summer 2002), 18–19.

CHAPTER 10
1. WHO Press Release 40, May 26, 1995.
2. Lawrence K. Attman, "Worst May Be Over in Zaire's Ebola Outbreak," *New York Times*, May 27, 1995.
3. David Bryant, "Youth and the Coming Revival," *In Concert*, Summer 1996, 1.
4. David Bryant, "Is This the Generation?" *Pray!*, September/October 1998, 10.
5. Bryant, "Youth and the Coming Revival," 1.
6. The Joint, http://www.joint.wikispaces.com.
7. Mike Higgs, "Lead Us, Join Us, or Get Out of the Way!" *Pray!*, September/October 1998, 19.
8. Higgs, 18–19.
9. Cheri Fuller and Ron Luce, *When Teens Pray* (Sisters, OR: Multnomah, 2002), 131–133.
10. Becky Fischer, *Redefining Children's Ministry in the 21st Century* (Bismarck, ND: Kids in Ministry International, 2005), 169–170.
11. Lila Terhune (Brownsville Assembly of God prayer coordinator), interview by Cheryl Sacks, 1997.
12. Esther Ilnisky speaker information sheet, 2007.
13. Kim Butts, interview by Arlyn Lawrence, October 2006.

ABOUT THE AUTHORS

CHERYL SACKS is a national conference speaker, prayer mobilizer, and local church prayer consultant. Her book *The Prayer Saturated Church*, a handbook for local church prayer leaders (NavPress), is igniting prayer in thousands of churches nationwide. A former school teacher and youth leader, Cheryl has a deep desire to see a fervency for prayer and the biblical foundations for prayer effectively passed on to the next generation. Cheryl and her husband, Hal, reside in Phoenix, AZ. They have a married daughter, Nicole.

ARLYN LAWRENCE is a writer, prayer leader — and the praying mom of five children, pre-teen through adult. A contributing editor for *Pray!* magazine, she writes a regular column for intercessors and also co-wrote and edited the *PrayKids! Teacher's Guide* (NavPress), a comprehensive curriculum for discipling and mentoring children in prayer. Arlyn has also been a homeschooling mom, Moms in Touch leader, youth leader, and children's ministry director. It is her heart to see parents and children transformed, equipped, and flourishing as dynamic, praying disciples of Jesus Christ. She and her husband, Doug, live with their family in Tacoma, WA.

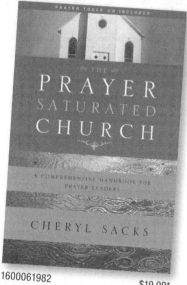

*Pray*K:ids!®

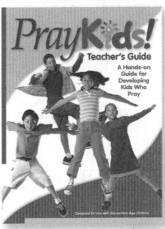

TEACH YOUR KIDS TO PRAY FOR THEIR WORLD...

KIDS' PRAYER CARDS

Teach Them to Pray Kingdom Prayers!

Praying for Government Leaders (#1600061818)

Praying for My Dad (#1600062032)

Praying for My Mom (#1600062024)

Praying for My Neighborhood (#1600060668)

Praying for My Pastor (#1600061826)

Praying for My School (#1600061834)

Praying for Myself (#160006065X)

$5* per pack of 20

...AND THE WHOLE WORLD...

T.H.U.M.B. PRAYER CARDS

T.H.U.M.B. Prayer Cards teach kids to pray for **T**ribal, **H**indu, **U**nreligious, **M**uslim, and **B**uddhist peoples around the world. One of each card per pack. (#1600061192)

$3* per pack

$2* per pack when purchasing 5 or more packs

PrayKids!®

Here's a resource to help you pray with more

Power, Passion, & Purpose

Every issue of *Pray!* will provide outstanding content:

• Powerful teaching by seasoned intercessors and prayer leaders

• Encouragement to help you grow in your prayer life—no matter at what level you are currently

• Exciting news stories on the prayer movement and prayer events around the world

• Profiles on people, organizations, and churches with unique prayer ministries

• Practical ideas to help you become a more effective prayer

• Inspirational columns to stimulate you to more passionate worship of Christ

• Classic writings by powerful intercessors of the past

• And much, much more!

No Christian who wants to connect with God should be without *Pray!*

Six issues of *Pray!*® are only $19.97*

(Canadian and international subscriptions are $25.97.)

*plus sales tax where applicable

Call **1-800-691-PRAY** (or 1-515-242-0297)
and mention code H5PRBKLTM when you place your order.

For information on other prayer tools, Bible studies, and prayer guides
call for a free prayer resource catalog: 719-531-3585.

INFUSE YOUR
YOUTH MINISTRY WITH
PASSIONATE PRAYER!

Is your youth ministry building prayer into the lives of tomorrow's leaders? *Youth Ministry on Your Knees* will help you and the young people you lead develop rich and effective prayer lives that will impact generations to come.

1-57683618-5 $12*

Pray! Books
ENCOURAGING A PASSION FOR
CHRIST THROUGH PRAYER

NAVPRESS
BRINGING TRUTH TO LIFE
www.navpress.com

TO ORDER CALL 1-800-366-7788 (7AM-5PM M-F, MST) or for international orders, call 1-719-548-9222.

Save 20% by ordering online at www.praymag.com

*plus postage/handling and applicable sales tax